We hope you [...]
memories of o[...]
you very much for your support.

*Justin Noice*

18 February 1994.

Managing Director
ICS Petroleum Ltd.

# BRITISH COLUMBIA

"British Columbia's Enterprises"
by Ruby Jaggernath

Produced in Co-operation with
the British Columbia Chamber of Commerce

Windsor Publications, Ltd.
Burlington, Ontario

"British Columbia's Enterprises"
by Ruby Jaggernath

# BRITISH COLUMBIA

## LAND OF RICH
## DIVERSITY

A CONTEMPORARY PORTRAIT

BY JUDITH ALLDRITT MCDOWELL AND JIM LYON

Windsor Publications, Ltd.—Book Division
Managing Editor: Karen Story
Design Director: Alexander E. D'Anca
Photo Director: Susan L. Wells
Executive Editor: Pamela Schroeder

Staff for *British Columbia*
Senior Editor: Teri Davis Greenberg
Photo Editor: Robin L. Sterling
Senior Editor, Corporate Profiles: Jeffrey Reeves
Production Editor, Corporate Profiles: Justin Scupine
Co-ordinator, Corporate Profiles: Gladys McKnight
Publisher's Representatives: M. Sorrenson, G. Jones
Editorial Assistants: Elizabeth Anderson, Alex
     Arredondo, Kate Coombs, Lori Erbaugh, Phyllis
     Feldman-Schroeder, Wilma Huckabey
Layout Artist, Corporate Profiles: Lisa Barrett
Layout Artist, Editorial: Bonnie Felt
Designer: Alex D'Anca

Windsor Publications, Ltd.
Elliot Martin, Chairman of the Board
James L. Fish III, Chief Operating Officer

LEFT: The majestic totem poles of Vancouver's Stanley Park celebrate British Columbia's rich heritage. Photo by Thomas Kitchin/First Light

PREVIOUS SPREAD: A golden blanket covers the hills of Vancouver Island near the charming village of Tofino. Photo by Ron Watts/First Light

# Contents

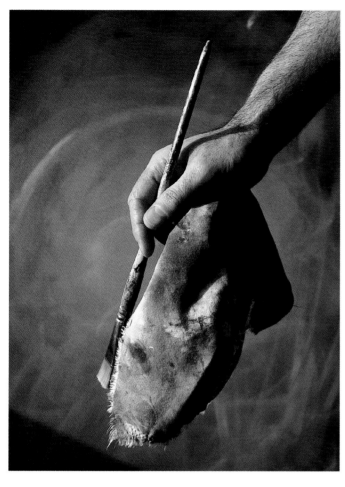

# PART ONE

# A Rich and Vital Land

Truly a rich and vital
land, British Columbia
has it all. Here, a soli-
tary hiker takes in the
grandeur of Yoho Na-
tional Park. Photo by
J.A. Kraulis/Masterfile

CHAPTER ONE

# Scenic
# Spectacular

by Judith Alldritt McDowell

B ritish Columbia, Canada's most westerly
province, covers an immense land area. Two
and a half times the size of Japan, four times
the size of Great Britain, and bigger than Germany, France, Austria, and Switzerland put
together, British Columbia is Canada's third-
largest province, after Quebec and Ontario.
Its surface area totals 947,000 square kilometres, nearly one-tenth the land mass of
Canada as a whole. In direct distances, B.C.
measures approximately 1,200 kilometres
north to south and averages about 600 kilometres east to west.

The province is shaped like a broad
snub-nosed boot with its heel in the Pacific
Ocean and its toe nudging the southwest corner of the province of Alberta. The top of the
boot touches the Alaska panhandle on the
west and the Yukon on the north. Its sole
rests on the northern borders of three American states: Washington, Idaho, and Montana.

This is a land of forest-clad, snow-capped
mountains, rushing rivers and rapids, semi-
arid deserts, fertile agricultural valleys, and a
long, intricate coastline dotted with idyllic islands, calm bays, marshy inlets, and densely
forested fjords.

**A lone backpacker
pauses during an
exhilarating hike in
Tweedsmuir Provin-
cial Park. The largest
of about 350 British
Columbian provincial
parks, Tweedsmuir
covers 9,811 square
kilometres on the east-
ern side of the Coast
Mountains. Photo by
Steve Short/First Light**

Apart from its spectacular coastline, the province's most characteristic natural feature is its mountains. Formed from volcanic upheavals of the earth's crust hundreds of millions of years ago, the mountains run the length and breadth of the province, covering a full three-quarters and more of the total surface area.

Although high plateaus cover most of the south-central interior and the northwest corner near the Yukon border, only the Peace River country in the northeast corner is a flatlands plain. The rest of the province is made up of several contiguous mountain ranges, including the Coast Mountains north from Vancouver; the Cassiar, Omineca, and Skeena mountains in the northern interior; the Purcell Mountains in the southeast corner; and the Rocky Mountains, running diagonally along the eastern edge of the province.

Along with the mountains are forests. British Columbia, the land of the big trees, is still largely covered with immense stands of Douglas fir, western red cedar, pine, spruce, and hemlock. Both along the coast and in the high country of the interior, evergreen forests dominate the landscape, creating some of the most beautiful scenery and finest recreation areas in the world.

That's the big picture. But within the immense territory that comprises British Columbia are several distinct geographic regions, each with its own particular landscape, economic structure, and way of life. Although all regions share the same language and government, they differ profoundly from one another in certain essential respects. To understand British Columbia, it is necessary to appreciate the unique character of each region, physically, culturally, and economically.

LEFT: A flight over Bella Coola provides a spectacular view of British Columbia's Coast Mountains. Running north-south along the western edge of the Interior Plateau, the Coast Mountains make up one of the province's six topographic regions. Photo by Gordon J. Fisher/First Light

FACING PAGE: The crystal-blue waters of Lake McArthur reflect the surrounding mountains of Yoho National Park. Photo by J.A. Kraulis/Masterfile

BELOW: A nature lover skillfully manoeuvres a canoe across Kappan Lake. Photo by Rick O'Neill/ First Light

### Vancouver Island and the Gulf Islands

On the west side of Georgia Strait, 32 kilometres from the southern coast of British Columbia, lies Vancouver Island, named for Captain George Vancouver, the British explorer who visited this part of the continent in 1792. With a land area roughly the size of Holland, Vancouver Island has a total population of approximately 550,000, concentrated mostly at Victoria and Nanaimo in the southern third of the island. Fishing and tourism are important industries in both north and south, but the central economic factor in this region is the presence of vast tracts of cedar and Douglas fir forest.

A spine of steep, rugged mountains runs the length of the island, separating the protected east side, where most of the roads, towns, and lumber and pulp mills are

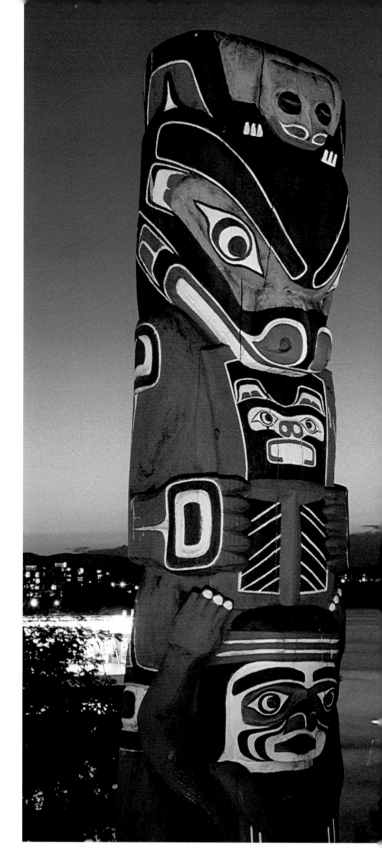

**ABOVE: Mist-enshrouded Long Beach is part of the Pacific Rim National Park, which is located on the Pacific coast of Vancouver Island. Photo by Mark Tomalty/Masterfile**

**PREVIOUS SPREAD: Boats docked at the picturesque fishing village of Tofino on Vancouver Island will soon set out in search of herring and other fish indigenous to the local waters. Photo by Thomas Kitchin/First Light**

**RIGHT: A totem pole appears to stand watch over the glittering lights of Victoria's Inner Harbor. The provincial capital of British Columbia, Victoria is an international tourist destination and a bustling commercial centre. Photo by F. Stuart Westmorland/Tom Stack & Associates**

located, from the ancient rain forests on the west coast. Here, where the open Pacific lashes the rocky shores and long tongues of sea water curl inland through narrow inlets and fjords, ocean mists shroud the tops of giant trees hundreds of years old, creating an atmosphere of primeval wilderness. One of the world's longest stretches of white-sand beach is located here, along with hundreds of smaller sandy beaches, remote bays, and rocky, offshore islands where seals and sea birds come to breed.

In another part of the island, only a couple of hundred miles to the south, a quarter of a million people enjoy the modern, sophisticated pleasures of life in Victoria, the provincial capital. Known the world over for the year-round beauty of its gardens, the mildness of

its climate, and the charm of its heritage cityscape, Victoria is more than just the seat of government for the province. It is also an international tourist destination and a bustling commercial centre with a large and prosperous retirement community.

Large car ferries carrying passengers and goods go back and forth many times a day from Vancouver Island to the mainland. Ferries also provide daily transportation to the Gulf Islands, an archipelago consisting of five major islands and hundreds of small islets that lie just off the east coast of Vancouver Island inside the protected waters of the Strait of Georgia.

Scenically, each one of these islands is a miniature

paradise with a special character all its own. Together they constitute an endless smorgasbord of sandy coves, rocky headlands, and quiet bays where curious sailors can happily lose themselves for weeks at a time.

Although the climate and landscape are similar to those of the lower mainland, life in the Gulf Islands has a relaxed, intimate quality, quite different from the flavor of life in Vancouver or Victoria. Once heavily agricultural, the Gulf Islands today are a favorite summer retreat for city people from the mainland. They are also home to thousands of year-round residents, including artists, fishermen, loggers, boat builders, and retirees from all parts of the country.

**Vancouver and the Lower Mainland**

Vancouver may not be as big as Los Angeles, as busy as Tokyo, or as historic as London, but for scenery it can hold its own with any city in the world.

Water and mountains dictate the shape of life in Vancouver, a city ringed by bays and inlets with a shoreline as irregular as the flight path of a bumble bee. From anywhere in the city, you have only to raise your eyes to see snow-capped mountain peaks. Looking out over the burly dockland of the downtown eastside or strolling serenely along the Stanley Park sea wall, you are constantly reminded that the ocean is never far away. You can see and feel its influence even on the farmland south

PREVIOUS SPREAD: A nighttime aerial view of Vancouver transforms the bustling city into a sparkling, illuminated blanket. Photo by Thomas Kitchin/First Light

FACING PAGE: Not all of Vancouver's visual appeal is in its natural wonders. Lions Gate Bridge, spanning Burrard Inlet from downtown Vancouver to the north shore, is one of the city's magnificent man-made structures. Photo by J.A. Kraulis/ Masterfile

RIGHT: Evening descends on peaceful Howe Sound near Squamish. Photo by J.A. Kraulis/ Masterfile

BELOW: Barns and silos dot the fertile, mountain-ringed farmland of the Fraser Valley, where dairy products, fruits, vegetables, and poultry are produced. Photo by Thomas Bruckbauer/First Light

of the city, where the silty waters of the Fraser River split up into several branches, meeting the ocean in a wide alluvial quilt stitched in a pattern of marshy islands.

Built at the edge of the wilderness on the site of a former sawmill, Vancouver looks its elegant best with the forest of office towers in the city center framed against a backdrop of snowy mountains and the blue waters of English Bay in the foreground. Surrounded by water on three sides, the center of the city rides between English Bay and Burrard Inlet like a giant barge strain-

ing at its tether. Close to the city center is Vancouver's residential "west end," the most densely occupied real estate outside of Hong Kong. The west end's backyard is Stanley Park, a unique combination of ocean beaches and 405 hectares of magnificent old-growth cedar and Douglas fir forest.

Vancouver is a uniquely livable city despite a decade or more of rapid growth and development. One of the city's livable attributes is its gardens. Vancouverites love gardens—all kinds of gardens—whether they are hanging gardens on the balconies of west end apartment towers, formal gardens at the entrance to Stanley Park, a tropical garden in Queen Elizabeth Park, demonstration gardens at the Van Dusen Botanical Gardens, the Sun Yat Sen Memorial Garden in Chinatown, or the Nitobe Japanese Garden at the University of B.C. All over the city, from early spring until the Christmas rains, lovingly tended home gardens are filled to bursting with the vibrant colors of rhododendrons, roses, and chrysanthemums. In winter flower stalls brighten nearly every street corner; in spring, the streets are frosty-pink with the fallen petals of Japanese cherry blossoms.

In winter it rains, and a chilly mist blankets the mountains above the city, drifting down and out across the cold, slate-colored sea. Then suddenly the low blanket of cloud lifts, and Vancouver sparkles in the sun like a freshly washed diamond. Sunlight glints off the snow-capped

north shore mountains and is reflected thousands of times in the mirrored walls of office towers and the windows of apartment buildings that line English Bay.

Out in the bay freighters wait silently at anchor with the bluffs of Spanish Banks and Point Grey behind them, their red hulls sitting high out of the water like toy boats on a pond. The bright sails of pleasure boats lift in the wind as they spin and glide gracefully back and forth across the bay.

Underneath the Lions Gate Bridge in Burrard Inlet, the north shore is dotted with yellow hills of sulphur and wood chips waiting to be loaded onto ships bound for the Pacific Rim. On the south shore at the foot of Granville Street, the white sails on the roof of Canada Place lift a greeting to the commerce of the world.

Vancouver is uniquely situated for scenery and commerce. Located at the western edge of a vast continent rich in natural resources, Vancouver looks across the Strait of Georgia toward the Pacific Rim and south toward the United States. Beyond the mountains to the east lie the grain-rich Canadian prairies and to the north, more mountains laden with coal and other minerals.

Virtually every kind of economic activity in the province, from farming, fishing, and forestry to manufacturing, tourism, and financial services, is represented in Vancouver and the lower mainland. Although this is the smallest region in the province, accounting for only 2.9

per cent of the total land area, 1.6 million people, more than half the population of British Columbia, live here.

Here are the headquarters for the giant forest and mining industries, the home of the Vancouver Stock Exchange, and the site of several major educational institutions, including the University of British Columbia and Simon Fraser University. The lower mainland is also the centre of British Columbia's cultural scene, the home of the Vancouver Symphony Orchestra, Ballet B.C., dozens of theatre companies, and four professional sports teams.

The lower mainland region includes the mountainous suburbs of North and West Vancouver on the north shore of Burrard Inlet and several small communities in the lower Fraser Valley, most of them within commuting distance of the city. Burnaby, Port Moody, Coquitlam,

and New Westminster occupy the hilly country east of Vancouver and north of the Fraser River. New Westminster is the oldest city on the mainland and the original capital of B.C.

The lowlands south of the city near the mouth of the Fraser River are largely agricultural. This is flat, rich, delta land, perfect for growing flowers and vegetables and raising horses and dairy cattle. Here also are located the burgeoning bedroom communities of Delta, Richmond, and Surrey. The 100-mile-long Fraser River delta extends south almost to the U.S. border, taking in the thriving centers of Chilliwack, Abbotsford, Langley, Cloverdale, Ladner, and Steveston, a fishing village founded by Japanese immigrants in the late nineteenth century.

In the marshy tidal estuaries at the mouth of the

While sailboats ride the winds off the Vancouver waterfront, majestic-looking mountains loom over the city's modern office towers. Photo by Al Harvey/ Masterfile

berry crops. Just north of Hope, the town of Yale marks the southern end of the Fraser Canyon, a spectacular river gorge with walls as high as 600 metres on either side that separates the interior regions of the province from the coast.

The combination of a thriving, sophisticated city surrounded by steep mountains, rugged ocean, and a broad river valley makes Vancouver and the lower mainland an exciting place to visit and a wonderful place to live.

### Howe Sound/Sunshine Coast

The rugged Coast Mountain Range extends north from Vancouver to the border with Alaska and west to the land's edge, rimming the Inside Passage with densely forested, nearly perpendicular granite slopes. These mountains contain several magnificent glaciers and the highest peaks in the province, including Mt. Garibaldi (2,670 metres), Mt. Waddington (4,017 metres), and Mt. Fairweather (4,663 metres) near the Alaska/Yukon border. Too rocky and steep for settlement of a serious kind, the Coast Ranges form a 100-mile-wide barrier between the populous lower mainland with its mild rain-coast climate and the dry mountainous plateau that covers the southern half of the B.C. interior.

The B.C. coastline from Horseshoe Bay a few miles north of Vancouver to Prince Rupert at the top of Hecate Strait is an intricate, scenic choreography of deep, narrow fjords, densely forested bays and inlets, sheer granite bluffs, boulder-strewn beaches, and a seemingly endless chain of rocky islands. Accessible for the most part only by boat or car ferry, the coastline is sparsely populated except for a few places where a pulp mill or a mine is located. The main industries along the coast are fishing, logging, and tourism.

At Horseshoe Bay, where the fjord known as Howe Sound slashes steeply and spectacularly inland, a handful of small islands in the mouth of the sound provide peaceful weekend retreats for frantic city dwellers. North from Horseshoe Bay, a winding, precipitous road follows the rim of Howe Sound to the town of Squamish, the Indian name for "birthplace of the winds." This is the gateway to the world-renowned Whistler/Blackcomb Mountain ski resort, part of Garibaldi National Park.

From here, ferries cross to Langdale near the colorful village of Gibson's Landing on the north side of the sound and to Nanaimo on the east coast of Vancouver

river, blue herons, nearly 200 species of migratory ducks, geese, sea birds, harbour seals, and other animals find refuge. In the summer grey whales pass by offshore and vast schools of salmon enter the mouth of the mighty Fraser River on their trek to remote spawning grounds hundreds of miles upstream. Meanwhile the beaches in coastal communities such as White Rock, Crescent Beach, and Tsawwassen attract a steady stream of sun and surf seekers from the city to the north.

Inland, the scenic, mountain-ringed farmlands and communities of the fertile Fraser River Valley extend eastward to Hope. Here, sleek dairy cattle graze in the shadow of high mountains on a flat, green plain dotted with giant barns and snub-nosed cattle-feed silos, and interspersed with lush fields of corn, peas, beans, and

Island 20 miles away. From Langdale, a combination of roads and ferries brings you to the resort town of Sechelt, then across Jervis Inlet and on northward to the fishing village of Lund at the entrance to Desolation Sound. This region, known locally as the "Sunshine Coast," is a favorite haunt of summertime sailors and pleasure boaters who return year after year to anchorages with such romantic names as Buccaneer Bay, Smuggler Cove, Secret Cove, Frenchman's Cove, and Welcome Passage.

## Okanagan

Best known for its orchards and vineyards and its hot, sunshine-filled summers, the Okanagan Valley, with its rolling hills, is a mecca for tourists from Alberta and the cooler, wetter parts of B.C. This Napa Valley of the north is also a water-sports wonderland whose attractions include sailing or water-skiing on gigantic Okanagan Lake and basking in the sun or angling for trout from the banks of countless smaller lakes and streams. Some people come to taste the fruit of the vine in the region's many estate wineries, and some come just to enjoy the lake-country scenery, including the springtime sights and scents of acres and acres of apple, peach, and cherry orchards in full bloom.

Enclosed by the Cascade Mountains to the west and the Monashee Mountains to the east, the Okanagan Valley occupies the southern tip of B.C.'s vast Interior Plateau and shares its southern border with the state of Washington. Although small in area, the region's climate, scenery, and semi-rural lifestyle have attracted a sizable population, most of which is concentrated around Okanagan Lake in towns such as Penticton, Kelowna, and Vernon, or at Princeton in the valley of the Similkameen River to the west. The population density is higher here than anywhere else outside the

PREVIOUS SPREAD: The sun beats down on snow-covered Mt. Seymour, one of the majestic peaks of the Coast Mountain Range. Mt. Seymour Provincial Park is located northeast of Vancouver. Photo by Patrick Morrow/First Light

RIGHT: The Okanagan Valley has attracted a sizable population in recent years due to the region's scenery, climate, and lifestyle. Best known for its orchards, vineyards, and hot summers, the Okanagan comprises 90 percent of British Columbia's viticulture industry. This apple orchard is located in the valley's community of Coldstream. Photo by Brian Sytnyk/ Masterfile

lower mainland or southern Vancouver Island.

The semi-arid river valleys of the Okanagan contain 90 per cent of the orchards and vineyards in the province, making agriculture a major element in the economy, but mining, forestry, sawmilling, and non-resource-based manufacturing employ more than twice as many people. Today young people in the Okanagan find employment in a variety of fields, including tourism and services related to a growing retirement community.

## Kootenay/Rocky Mountains

The Selkirks, the Purcells, and the Monashee—for people in southeastern British Columbia, these names mean magic, the magic of mountains. They conjure up images of sky-blue lakes and emerald valleys, of hot springs and ice fields, of snow-packed ski hills and densely forested wilderness trails.

The names belong to a series of steep, north/south mountain ranges that lie parallel to one another north of the U.S. border in the southeast corner of B.C. in the region known as Kootenay country. This is a triangle-shaped, ruggedly mountainous area that takes its name from long and narrow Kootenay Lake, which stretches north and south for more than 100 miles in the valley between the Selkirk and Purcell ranges north of Creston

and just above the border with Idaho. West of the Selkirks and east of the Monashee range, the two Arrow Lakes (upper and lower) are even thinner than Kootenay Lake and just as long.

Between these lakes is the Slocan Valley, home of Slocan Lake and two spectacular wilderness areas—the Valhalla and Kokanee Glacier provincial parks. In the Rocky Mountains to the east, the Columbia River starts its journey to the coast, forming a beautiful, open valley surrounded by the towering, glaciated peaks of the Rockies and the forested wilderness slopes of the Purcell Mountains.

Mining, first for silver and gold and then for lead, zinc, and coal, opened this area to settlement in the late 1800s. Mining and smelting have always been primary industries here, and coal mining is still the main economic activity in the eastern part of the region around Fernie. However, forestry (including logging and wood processing) is even more important. Tourism, based on skiing in the winter and a variety of outdoor recreation activities in the summer, has been gaining in economic significance throughout the region. Also important economically are the dams and hydro-electric power generating facilities in the deep valleys of the west Kootenays on the upper waterways of the mighty Columbia River.

## Cariboo

This is British Columbia's cattle country, a high-mountain plateau made up largely of rolling, semi-arid hills and sagebrush-covered plains dotted with rocky mesas. Named for the Cariboo Mountains in the northeastern corner of the region, this relatively horizontal landscape is a welcome sight to tourists who have just negotiated some heart-thumping stretches of the Fraser Canyon or Coquihalla highways, the only two modern highways to the interior from the southern coast.

Stretching from the eastern slopes of the Coast Mountains across most of the width of the province, the Cariboo takes up 13 per cent of the province's total land area and a huge chunk of the central Interior Plateau. The Fraser River runs like a spine through the centre of the region, creating a string of river and lakeside communities, including the important sawmilling and administrative centres of Williams Lake and Quesnel.

Although the valleys are burned brown in summer, the Cariboo is not all dry stones and bones. Fed by melting mountain snows sheltered among the forests of spruce and fir found high on the mountain slopes from both the east and west, the mighty Thompson and Fraser rivers bring life to the land, cutting deep, rapid-filled canyons and spreading an octopus-like network of streams and lakes to nourish the range grasses. On the east the land climbs up to meet the spectacular glacial scenery of Wells Gray Provincial Park.

ABOVE: The Vermilion River runs through Kootenay National Park, one of the province's several national parks. The park runs along the Continental Divide of the Canadian Rockies, which borders on the neighboring province of Alberta. Photo by Thomas Kitchin/First Light

FACING PAGE: Weary hikers take in the view from Red Line Creek in the Purcell Mountains. The Purcells, part of the Columbia Mountains, are located between the Selkirks and the Rockies in the southeast region of British Columbia. Photo by Patrick Morrow/First Light

Largely as a result of its tempestuous past, the Cariboo has a reputation for being wild and woolly. Penetrated by fur traders in the eighteenth century, the region was opened up by the gold fever that hit the Fraser Canyon in 1858. Settlements such as 100 Mile House and 150 Mile House are left over from the 1860s when stagecoaches full of thirsty prospectors stopped frequently to change horses during the bone-rattling, 48-hour journey along the Cariboo Wagon Road from the head of navigation at Yale to the saloons and gold mines of Barkerville.

Although panning for gold has largely gone the way of the stagecoach, gold, silver, copper, and molybdenum mining are still part of the economic picture in the

region. The forest industry is the largest single employer today, while the southern half of the region remains the centre of cattle ranching in British Columbia. This area boasts some of North America's largest cattle ranches, including the fabled Douglas Lake Ranch near Williams Lake.

## North by Northwest

This vast and sparsely populated region covers almost a third of the province, including the northern end of British Columbia's rolling Interior Plateau, the remotely beautiful and heavily forested Queen Charlotte Islands, and mile upon mile of rugged, unspoiled mountain wilderness in the northwest corner of the province.

Although the area is rich with wildlife and magnificent scenery, relatively few tourists penetrate this far north. The main economic activities are sawmilling, pulp and paper manufacturing, and mining. However, fishing and fish processing are also critical to the life of coastal communities such as Prince Rupert.

The transportation hub of the region is Prince George, located in the southeast corner at the junction of the Fraser and Nachako rivers. From here, road and rail lines flow north, south, east, and west through a wide variety of landscape, from open meadows and tree-covered hills to rivers and lakes practically seething with trout and other game fish.

The well-known Yellowhead Highway bisects the region, running parallel to the Canadian National Railway tracks from the Alberta border near Jasper, through the lake country west of Prince George all the way to the port of Prince Rupert, which is also accessible by ferry from Vancouver Island. Another highway branches off north through the scenic Stikine Ranges to Stewart (the most northerly ice-free port in Canada) on the Alaska border and on through the Cassiar Mountains to the Yukon.

Most people live on farms or in small, friendly communities strung out many miles apart along the main highways. Outside these relatively settled areas, the region is dotted with isolated homesteads and remote mining or logging camps whose only access is by dirt road, float plane, or helicopter. Despite the cruelly cold, snowbound winters and short, insect-ridden summers, there are few regions of the continent more satisfying to lovers of natural beauty and true wilderness.

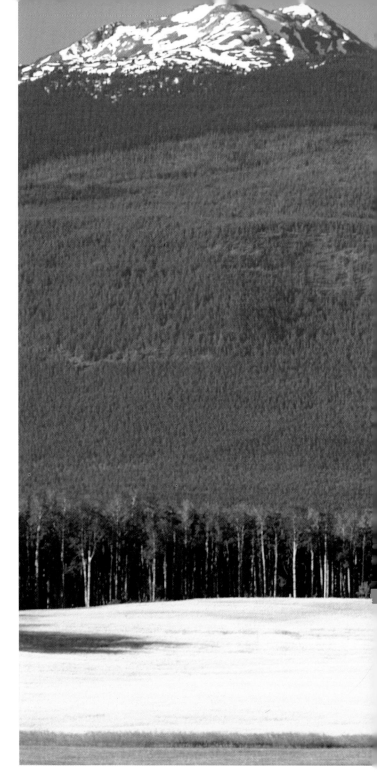

## Peace River Country

The graceful, fertile plains of the Peace River Valley have been carved by the majestic Peace River flowing east toward Alberta from its headwaters near sprawling Williston Lake behind the massive Bennett Dam and hydro-electric power plant. This immense area in the northeast corner of the province is a different world from the rugged mountain wilderness to the northwest. Although bounded on the west by the Rocky Mountains and criss-crossed by mighty rivers, much of the terrain here is flat, suitable for growing grain and raising beef cattle.

Despite a short growing season less than half as long as in the southern regions of the province, the lush farms of the Peace River country produce mighty harvests of wheat and oats for the hungry markets of the world. Since the 1950s, oil and natural gas exploration and

development have added to the economic base in the region. Within the last decade, one of the most modern strip coal mines in the world has been opened on Quintette Mountain southwest of Dawson Creek near the instant town of Tumbler Ridge.

The world-famous Alaska Highway cuts diagonally through the region for 960 kilometres, from Dawson Creek on the Alberta border through Fort St. John and Fort Nelson to the Yukon border. The Canadian and U.S. military built the highway in just nine months in response to a feared Japanese invasion in 1942. Thanks to the highway, now paved most of the way, some of the finest wilderness landscape in North America has been opened up to travellers willing to risk a few hazards for the opportunity to witness the scenic spectacles along this unique route.

ABOVE: The home of some of North America's largest cattle ranches, the Cariboo region is a high-mountain plateau of rolling hills and plains. Here, nature has placed a blanket of lush greenery at the foot of the Cariboo Mountains near Dunster in the northeastern corner of the region. Photo by J.A. Kraulis/Masterfile

FACING PAGE: The 960-kilometre Alaska Highway passes through some of North America's most beautiful wilderness. The Canadian and U.S. military built the highway in just nine months in 1942 in response to a feared Japanese invasion. Photo by Hans Blohm/Masterfile

# By Air, Land, and Water

by Jim Lyon

B ecause of its varied terrain and vast geography, British Columbia's transportation needs are unusually diverse.

Distances are so great and communities so widely dispersed that business travel in British Columbia is usually by air. The trip from downtown Vancouver to the capital city of Victoria, for example, takes little more than half an hour by float plane or helicopter compared to about four hours by a combination of car and ferry. The quick trip by air is favored by most businessmen, politicians, and bureaucrats.

British Columbians rely so much on air travel, in fact, that the province has one of the busiest air transportation systems in Canada, with 376 airports, airstrips, and float plane facilities serving more than 11 million passengers each year.

Highway travel has improved remarkably since the 1950s thanks mainly to the government of the late W.A.C. Bennett, whose road-building activities to "open up" the interior of the province were conducted with almost evangelical fervor.

Today, despite the vast distances, difficult terrain, and the fear of rock slides, avalanches,

A region of varied terrain and expansive geography, British Columbia's challenging transportation needs are met by air, water, highway, and rail.  B.C. Ferries, one of the world's largest ferry operators, carried 19.2 million passengers in 1989-1990. Photo by Edward M. Gifford/Masterfile

and road washouts on some highways, British Columbia enjoys a healthy transportation system that is still evolving as the provincial economy expands and matures.

Vancouver harbor is a constant hive of activity. Fast ferries, called SeaBus, flit across the water from the downtown commercial core to North Vancouver; huge bulk carriers conveying grain, forest products, and sulphur slip under the Lions Gate suspension bridge (built, incidentally, by Ireland's Guinness brewing family) and out into the open Pacific, headed mostly for the Orient; elegant cruise ships turn north to see the glaciers of Alaska; and float planes buzz overhead constantly.

The Port of Vancouver is Canada's largest port and the second biggest in North America in terms of foreign tonnage. It also ranks among the top 20 ports in the world.

Today the port encompasses more than 219 kilometres of coastline. Burrard Inlet, the major centre of activity, extends 28 kilometres along the north and south shores to Port Moody. Roberts Bank, built just north of the United States border and 37 kilometres south of Vancouver, is the site of the largest, deepwater coal-handling facility in North America.

The first export cargo, a shipment of lumber and fence pickets bound for Australia, was shipped from

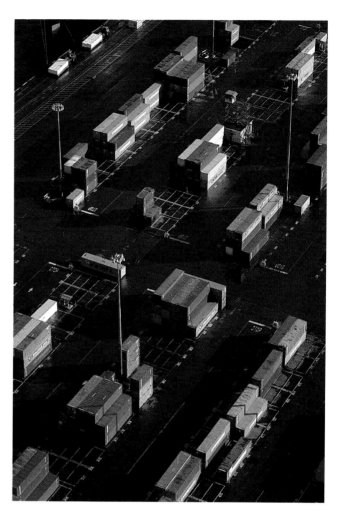

LEFT: The Port of Vancouver, which is the province's major seaport, is a constant hub of activity. Photo by Thomas Kitchin/ First Light

ABOVE: The container docks of the Port of Vancouver contribute to the efficient handling of a wide variety of cargoes. Photo by Gordon J. Fisher/First Light

Moodyville in North Vancouver in 1864. One hundred twenty-five years later the port handled more than 64 million tonnes of cargo. Bulk shipments, mostly Western Canadian resource commodities, accounted for 85.6 per cent of this tonnage. The most significant of these were coal and coke (23.8 million metric tonnes), grain (9.2 million tonnes), sulphur (4.5 million tonnes), potash (3.5 million tonnes), and wood chips (2 million tonnes).

All this activity requires the Canadian Coast Guard's Vancouver Traffic Centre to monitor between 225,000 and 250,000 vessels a year, from fishing boats and general freighters to the 100,000-tonne-plus leviathans that load coal at the Roberts Bank Superport. The Coast Guard's count does not include an estimated 250,000 pleasure boats that ply the waters around Vancouver and Vancouver Island.

In total, the Port of Vancouver handles close to 10,000 vessel calls each year, of which 3,000 are foreign vessels representing Canada's Pacific Coast trade with 40 nations.

Loading and discharging cargo takes place at 29 terminals with a full range of deepwater facilities and services. Most are situated in the inner harbor, extending from Lions Gate Bridge and encircling both the north and south shores of Burrard Inlet. These include: two coal and five grain terminals, two container terminals, five specialized-cargo terminals, five mineral and petroleum terminals, four forest-product terminals, and two cruise ship terminals.

The Port of Vancouver boasts that all cargo terminals

travelling in or out of Vancouver each season has more than doubled from 140,000 in the late 1970s to more than 300,000 today. This is welcome business for Vancouver since the ships and their passengers spend an estimated $66 million to $85 million in the city.

Burrard Inlet has also doubled as an airport since 1931, when the first float planes began landing there. With its own control tower, it sees an average of 5,000 take-offs and landings a month.

The northern British Columbia coast boasts another excellent harbor at Prince Rupert, about 700 kilometres north of Vancouver. The large, ice-free, naturally deep harbor offers protection for vessels up to 250,000 dead-weight tonnes. The port's location, just south of the Alaskan Panhandle, is an important factor for shipping companies since the distance between Prince Rupert and Asian-Pacific ports is shorter by about 420 nautical miles than to any other North American West Coast port. This means a day less transit time in each direction. The port is served by the Canadian National Railway's northern main line.

The Port of Prince Rupert offers facilities for lumber, pulp, coal, grain, and general cargo shipments. In 1989 it shipped 11.3 million metric tonnes of cargo, more than half of which was metallurgical coal, almost all of it bound for Japan. Wheat shipments (almost 1.8 million tonnes) included exports to Iran, Jordan, the People's Republic of China, and the Soviet Union. During 1989 the harbor recorded a total of 1,705 calls by vessels of all types, including deep-sea cargo carriers, tugs, barges, ferries, and cruise ships.

The British Columbia ferry fleet is one of the largest in the world. It is also among the most popular. During 1989-1990 the ferry system carried 19.2 million passengers and 7.5 million vehicles.

B.C. Ferries, a provincially owned and operated Crown Corporation, provides passenger and vehicle service to 42 ports of call along the coast. Its 38 vessels operate on 25 routes to carry residents, visitors, business travellers, and bus and commercial vehicle operators.

The ferry system is a vital sea link between the B.C. mainland and the many islands dotted along the coast of Canada's westerly province.

Today's distinctive red, white, and blue ferries range in size from the huge 457-foot-long "Cowichan" class vessels that carry 1,500 passengers and 362 vehicles to the small *Dogwood Princess*, which is just 42 feet long and

FACING PAGE, TOP: Cruise ships and their passengers spend an estimated $66 million to $85 million in the city due in part to the spectacular cruise terminal in downtown Vancouver's Canada Place complex. Photo by Ken Straiton/First Light

ABOVE: Almost every day between May and September sleek cruise ships such as this one can be seen leaving or entering Vancouver's harbor. Photo by Robert Semeniuk/First Light

FACING PAGE, BOTTOM: Making headway along its appointed route, a B.C. Ferry proudly displays the Canadian flag. Photo by Thomas Bruckbauer/First Light

offer the on-dock trackage of major railways plus excellent access to highways and Vancouver International Airport.

One of the port's most spectacular success stories has been the development of the Alaska cruise industry. Almost daily, during the May to September season, sleek, modern vessels, accommodating anywhere from 400 to 1,500 passengers, can be seen leaving or entering the harbor. Most noticeable are the Princess line vessels, familiar to millions through the popular "Loveboat" television series.

Vancouver has now become one of the world's busiest summer cruise ports. The two cruise terminals (including the truly spectacular one in the Canada Place complex in the heart of downtown) accommodate nearly 200 sailings each year. The number of cruise passengers

carries 38 passengers and no vehicles.

It is impossible to travel between the Tsawwassen ferry terminal south of Vancouver to Swartz Bay on Vancouver Island without admiring the quick efficiency with which the ferries are turned around. Within minutes of arriving at the terminals, hundreds of passenger cars, campers, trucks, busses, and foot passengers disembark from the vessels. As soon as the *Queen of Esquimalt, Queen of Saanich, Queen of Victoria,* and *Queen of Vancouver* are emptied, another tide of travellers swarms on board for the one hour, 35-minute crossing.

As they settle into the lounges or walk around the upper decks, passengers can focus their binoculars on the nearby Roberts Bank Superport, where bulk carriers, floating leviathans, are loading coal to fuel the steel mills of Japan and Korea. There are many other sights to attract the traveller's attention: pleasure yachts, fishing vessels, sometimes even a whale.

There's excitement too as the ferries slow down to manoeuvre through a narrow body of water called Active Pass. It is here, just about halfway through the voyage, that the big ferries travelling in opposite directions must pass each other in the constricted water between Mayne and Galiano islands. They sound their loud sirens imperiously to shoo smaller vessels out of their way. On-deck passengers feel they can almost reach out

and touch the rocky shoreline, so closely do the westward-bound ferries hug the southern shore of Galiano.

The ferries that operate on the 30-mile run from Horseshoe Bay in West Vancouver to Nanaimo on mid-Vancouver Island are curious-looking vessels with bow and bridge superstructures at each end of the ship. After docking at one of the terminals, the ship's master and helmsman simply walk to the bridge at the other end of the vessel. When it's time to pull away from the dock, they head out directly into the Strait of Georgia without fuss and the need to turn the ship around.

The popularity of ferry travel in recent years has

ABOVE: Two jets await takeoff at Vancouver International, where Air Canada, Canadian Airlines International, and many major foreign airlines provide service to British Columbia's travellers. Photo by J.A. Kraulis/ Masterfile

RIGHT: These brightly colored seaplanes operate out of the Seal Cove seaplane base in Prince Rupert. Photo by Thomas Kitchin/ First Light

FACING PAGE: Operated by B.C. Transit, SeaBus is a 400-passenger, catamaran-style ferry constructed of lightweight aluminum that has a cruising speed of 11.5 knots. It was introduced in 1977 as an alternate way to get from downtown Vancouver to the north shore across Burrard Inlet. Photo by Gary Fiegehen/First Light

strained the capacity of the fleet and its terminal facilities. To better accommodate the vast throngs of passengers, the ferry corporation is planning major terminal modifications intended to improve customer facilities and traffic flow as well as providing more parking space and larger holding areas.

An estimated $34 million was being spent to accommodate bigger ferries at Swartz Bay, improve marshalling

areas and parking lots, and relocate buildings and ticket booths. Highway access to the terminal and docking facilities was also being improved at Tsawwassen.

Two larger ships, known as S-Class vessels, are also planned for the Swartz Bay-Tsawwassen service by the mid-1990s. Each will be able to carry 470 automobiles.

British Columbia's ferry system is essentially an extension of the province's highway network. For this reason, the ferries are subsidized by the provincial government. Users, in fact, only pay about 87 per cent of the fleet's operating costs. The ferries link small rural communities, fishing ports, tourist attractions, and major forest-products complexes.

For those who appreciate life on board ship, B.C. Ferries offers a chance to enjoy two days of spectacular scenery on the 548-nautical-mile round-trip voyage through the Inside Passage between Port Hardy on Vancouver Island and Prince Rupert on the north mainland coast. The ship sails the 274-mile one-way route in 15 hours, stopping overnight at the opposite port and returning the next day to the passengers' original port of departure. The towns of Port Hardy and Prince Rupert are accessible by highway, daily coach service, and air service. In 1990 round-trip passengers could book overnight cabins for about $69 to $100 (U.S. dollars), depending on the type of cabin. The *Queen of the North* sails northward from Port Hardy on all even-numbered days in July and September and odd days in August. The return trip from Prince Rupert is on odd-numbered days in July and September and even days in August.

At Vancouver International Airport the big jets, tails as tall as apartment buildings, parade their national origins: Cathay Pacific, from Hong Kong; Lufthansa, from Germany; Qantas, from Australia; and British Airways. There are other foreign carriers too: Japan Air Lines, Korean Air, Air China, Air New Zealand, Singapore International, KLM Royal Dutch Airlines. And there are the neighborly Americans: Continental, Delta, American, United, and Federal Express.

Above all, Vancouver International is the home of Canada's two big flag carriers, and visitors will see mostly the distinctive markings of Air Canada and Canadian Airlines International, which fly extensively across Canada and also on many international routes. Also to be seen are many of the smaller aircraft of the very active feeder lines, AirBC and Time Air, which operate modestly sized turbo-prop aircraft to smaller communities in British Columbia and elsewhere in Western Canada.

In 1989 Vancouver International, Canada's second-busiest airport, handled 9.3 million passengers, 118,000 tonnes of air cargo, and 325,000 total aircraft movements.

There were 19 jet flights a day to Eastern Canada, about 170 flights a day to destinations across Western Canada, and 41 scheduled departures a week across the Pacific by eight international carriers. There were also 33 departures a week to Europe and frequent daily services to and from United States destinations with direct service to Seattle, Portland, San Francisco, San Jose, Los Angeles, Honolulu, Spokane, Denver, and Chicago.

With this volume of activity, Vancouver International (known in the aviation business as YVR) is already straining its capacity. Demands on its facilities are likely

ABOVE: Snow-capped Mt. Cheam towers over a stretch of the Trans-Canada Highway near Hope. Photo by Edward M. Gifford/ Masterfile

ABOVE RIGHT: A computer-controlled, driverless, light rapid transit system, Sky-Train travels at a cruising speed of 80 kilometres an hour in the Greater Vancouver area. Photo by Edward M. Gifford/ Masterfile

FACING PAGE: Sky-Train crosses the Fraser River on a new 616-metre-long bridge, the world's longest cable-stayed bridge designed solely for carrying rapid transit. Photo by Thomas Kitchin/First Light

to increase. Annual passenger volume is forecast to reach almost 15 million by the year 2001, a 60 per cent increase from 1989. In the same period, aircraft movements are expected to rise to 422,000, a 30 per cent increase.

Interestingly, burgeoning Pacific Rim routes produced a 34 per cent increase in heavy, wide-bodied aircraft between 1987 and 1989.

Because of mounting runway congestion in recent years, Transport Canada has proposed the construction of a new 9,940-foot runway, parallel to and 1.7 kilometres north of the existing main runway. This project, first discussed in the late 1940s, is subject to the federal government's Environmental Assessment and Review Process. If approved, construction of the new runway could begin in mid-1992 and would take about 19 months to complete.

Mounting congestion and delays at Vancouver International is of concern both provincially and nationally. The airport is both Canada's principal western hub for domestic aviation activity and the country's chief international gateway for trade with Pacific Rim nations and tourism.

Operating a major international airport on Sea Island in the Fraser River delta, 12 kilometres south of Vancouver, presents special challenges. The airport is surrounded by a sensitive and unique ecosystem. The estuary and foreshore areas are an extensive habitat for many forms of wildlife. The river provides the world's largest salmon run and the estuary supports Canada's greatest population of migrating and wintering waterfowl and shore birds. To protect the wildlife the airport takes special measures to guard against spills and has installed state-of-the-art water quality monitoring stations to monitor YVR's storm water run-off into the Fraser estuary.

Avoiding collisions between birds and aircraft is a particular concern since no comparable site along the Pacific Coast between Alaska and California supports the diversity and number of birds found in the Fraser delta. A wildlife management program has reduced the number of bird strikes from 107 in 1983 to 19 in 1989. Wildlife control specialists use various dispersement techniques to discourage birds from nesting and roosting on airport structures and operational services.

Coquitlam in the northeast.

The modern SeaBus, which made its first appearance in 1977, is the successor to a series of harbor ferries that had shuttled across Burrard Inlet from downtown Vancouver to the north shore for more than half a century. The two fast, 400-passenger, catamaran-style SeaBus ferries were introduced in response to demand for some sort of "third crossing" of the Inlet, to supplement the Lions Gate and Second Narrows bridges. Constructed of lightweight aluminum, the vessels have a cruising speed of 11.5 knots. Highly manoeuvrable, the double-ended ferries can move in any direction and turn in their own length. They depart every 15 minutes in each direction during daytime.

One of the most popular methods of transportation in the Greater Vancouver area is SkyTrain, a computer-controlled, driverless, light rapid transit system whose cars zip along at a cruising speed of 80 kilometres an hour. Because it travels on its own track, mostly high above street level, SkyTrain avoids traffic congestion and can carry large numbers of passengers at high speeds. It carries 90,000 riders every weekday.

Just over a century ago the first street cars began operating in Vancouver and Victoria. Today BC Transit vehicles carry more than 130 million people a year in three dozen communities throughout the province. The fleet consists of more than 800 diesel and trolley buses, 114 SkyTrain cars, and two SeaBus ferries in Greater Vancouver, along with 113 diesel buses in Victoria.

The Vancouver Regional Transit System covers about 1,500 square kilometres and, as such, is the largest transit service area in Canada. The area extends from Lions Bay in the northwest to Langley in the southeast, White Rock and the United States in the south, and Port

The first phase of SkyTrain—a 22-kilometre line between Burrard Inlet and New Westminster—was opened for service in January 1986 at a capital cost of $854 million. Fortunately, in downtown Vancouver it was possible to adapt and enlarge a disused railway tunnel for SkyTrain use. If it had been necessary to dig a new tunnel, it would have added $100 million to SkyTrain's cost.

To run SkyTrain south across the Fraser River it was necessary to build a massive new bridge. This structure, 616 metres long, was built at a cost of $129.5 million and is the world's longest cable-stayed bridge designed solely for carrying rapid transit. It has been designed to

ABOVE: A heavily laden logging truck crosses one of British Columbia's 2,700 bridges. Photo by Toby Rankin/Masterfile

FACING PAGE: A Canadian Pacific Railway train is dwarfed by Mt. Stephen near Field as it makes its way to its final destination. Photo by Wilhelm Schmidt/ Masterfile

resist wind gusts as high as 350 kilometres an hour and to survive the worse earthquake likely to hit the Lower Mainland.

SkyTrain crossed the Fraser River on the new bridge to the new Scott Road Station in Surrey in March 1990. This new link eases traffic congestion on the highway bridges and has cut in half the commuter time from Surrey, the Lower Mainland's fastest-growing community, to downtown Vancouver.

In 1989 the provincial government announced a one billion-dollar rapid transit construction program for Greater Vancouver. By the mid-1990s SkyTrain will be extended another four kilometres to Whalley Town Centre.

The government's program also included a rapid transit connection between downtown Vancouver and Richmond Town Centre, with a possible spur to Vancouver International Airport. It is projected that this rapid transit line will carry about 50,000 passengers a day when it is finished.

Another SkyTrain extension, this one to Lougheed Mall on the Burnaby-Coquitlam border, is expected to be completed in the late 1990s.

The provincial government has also announced the purchase of articulated SuperBuses for use on major transit corridors.

Also planned is a third SeaBus across Vancouver Harbor (to increase departure frequency to every 10 minutes) and possibly a high-speed passenger ferry between Port Moody, at the head of Burrard Inlet, and the downtown Vancouver SeaBus terminal.

A study by the provincial government shows that there are 47,060 kilometres of provincial highways in British Columbia. For those who enjoy statistics it's perhaps worth noting that of these, 22,000 kilometres are paved and 25,000 are gravelled. The province's roads traverse some of the toughest terrain in the country. There are 2,700 bridges, 165,000 culverts, 104,000 sign posts, and an additional 19,000 kilometres of roads under municipal jurisdiction. The message is clear: British Columbia is a large jurisdiction with a highway system that is still being developed.

The provincial government has pledged to continue a high level of funding for upgrading of major trunk routes.

British Columbia is also served by an extensive railway system. Indeed, railways have done much to define the province's population centres as they exist today. Vancouver, for example, developed specifically in response to the decision by the Canadian Pacific Railway to establish its western terminus on the shores of Burrard Inlet, at the site of the present downtown business core, rather than at the Inlet's eastern extremity at Port Moody, its first choice.

There are 5,415 kilometres of main line railway tracks in British Columbia. When spur lines are added, the total rises to 7,500 kilometres. Five major railways operate in the province: Canadian National, Canadian Pacific, British Columbia Railway, Burlington Northern, and the Southern Railway of BC (formerly BC Hydro Rail).

The railways in British Columbia are involved mainly in moving freight. In 1987 they transported a fifth of the tonnage moved in all of Canada and unloaded a third of the total Canadian freight. Much of this was coal—many millions of tonnes of it—extracted from mines in the Rocky Mountains of British Columbia and in neighboring Alberta and conveyed hundreds of miles to the West Coast for export.

Coal export is handled with remarkable efficiency. CP Rail, for example, operates "unit trains" from the coal fields in southeast B.C. to the deepwater ocean port at Roberts Bank. Each train hauls about 10,300 tonnes of coal in high-capacity gondola cars. Up to 18 train sets work a continuous cycle, taking about 88 hours to complete the 2,240-kilometre journey from mine to port and back to the mine.

Travelling snake-like over some of Canada's most rugged terrain, the 112-car trains heading west require up to five, 3,000-horsepower locomotives to make the trip through the mountains. Each car in the unit train is fitted with rotary couplers to accommodate the specially designed unloading equipment used at Roberts Bank. As the train moves through the unloading station, each car is gripped at both ends by a huge circular dumper and turned upside down. As the gondola car is turned, the coupler becomes the hub of the giant wheel formed by the rotating dumper. In as little as two hours, the entire train is unloaded. The empty train then promptly returns to the mine.

CP Rail's unit trains unload at Roberts Bank in a continuous procedure. The coal is moved by conveyor directly to ship or storage. The port can accommodate vessels up to 250,000 dead-weight tonnes and, with an annual capacity of 22.4 million metric tonnes, it is the largest coal port on the West Coast of North America.

The difficulties posed by British Columbia's rugged terrain are well illustrated by CP Rail's remarkable Rogers Pass Project, built at a cost of $500 million and completed in late 1988. Rogers Pass, in the heart of the Selkirk Mountains, was discovered in 1881 by Major Albert Bowman

LEFT: Five major railways operate in B.C.—Canadian National, Canadian Pacific, British Columbia, Southern Railway of BC, and Burlington Northern. Here, a Canadian Pacific train snakes its way through the spectacular Thompson River Canyon. Photo by John de Visser/ Masterfile

ABOVE: The freight trains of British Columbia's extensive railway network move more than a fifth of all tonnage in Canada along some 7,500 kilometres of track. Photo by Thomas Kitchin/ First Light

Rogers. It is a narrow, heavily forested pathway that rises to more than 1,300 metres above sea level in the midst of mountains towering more than 3,300 metres.

When the first rail line was laid through the pass in 1885, it looped back and forth along the sides of mountains, crossing creeks and ravines on massive wooden trestles. The line often fell victim to avalanches.

The pass averages more than 1,000 centimetres of snow annually and, today, Parks Canada and the Canadian Armed Forces trigger avalanches using artillery fire.

In 1916 CP Rail opened the eight-kilometre Connaught Tunnel, which avoided the worst of the avalanche paths, eliminated many of the worst curves, and reduced the rail summit by 168 metres. But there still remained the tough climb along the Beaver River Valley to the Connaught Tunnel. In just 13 kilometres, the line rises 275 metres, a steep climb for freight trains. To alleviate

this, CP Rail began construction of a second main line through the pass in 1984. This project was the largest construction undertaking of its kind by the railway since completion of the Trans-continental line in 1885.

The project included 17 kilometres of surface route, six bridges, and two tunnels, one of which at 14.7 kilometres is the longest railway tunnel in the Western Hemisphere. The work went on for four and a half years and at one point employed 1,100 people. The cost was almost $15 million a kilometre, which, CP Rail says, may make it the most expensive section of railway track in the world. The company says, though, that it's worth every last nickel, and it's easy to see why: The new line increases the railway's capacity to the West Coast by 60 per cent.

This has been done by reducing the westbound grade trains must climb from 2.2 per cent to a maximum of one per cent. The reduced grade eliminates the need to add six 3,000-horsepower pusher locomotives to each westbound train. Now the railway can move 24 trains west through the pass every day instead of the previous 15 and can use the old track for eastbound trains.

The Rogers Pass project is the latest example of the extraordinary efforts and considerable expenditures that have been made to give British Columbia a modern, efficient transportation network.

# Business B.C. Style

by Jim Lyon

I t has been said that Vancouver is the easiest, most pleasant Canadian city in which to do business. The deals are no more favorable and the negotiations no less tough, but the atmosphere, the climate in which discussions are conducted, lacks the frenetic compulsion to "do a deal" that is part of the business attitude in Calgary, Toronto, Montreal, and other cities.

People love visiting Vancouver to conduct business. Part of the reason is the climate. When the rest of Canada is gripped in winter's frigid embrace, it's nice to jump on a plane and leave behind the blizzards and icy roads and cars that won't start and walk by the ocean and look at daffodils in golden splendor.

Many business visitors attend sessions at the Vancouver Trade and Convention Centre, a large modern facility built on a pier sticking out into Burrard Inlet from which cruise ships bound for Alaska sail most days in the summer and fall.

British Columbia's location and sophisticated communications technology are now taken almost for granted by the province's businesses, large and small. Virtually instant voice and/or facsimile print contact can be made daily with business colleagues in Pacific Rim countries including Australia, Central and South America, Eastern Canada, the United Kingdom, and all of Europe.

The modern office towers of Vancouver's dynamic skyline reflect the vibrant economy and thriving business community of British Columbia. Photo by Thomas Kitchin/Tom Stack & Associates

FACING PAGE: Immense log booms such as these at Gambier Island, Howe Sound, will eventually end up under the blade in British Columbia sawmills. Photo by Gordon J. Fisher/First Light

ABOVE: A MacDonald Bay faller working in a verdant sea of foliage wields a heavy chainsaw as he begins to cut down a forest giant. Photo by Sherman Hines/Masterfile

PREVIOUS SPREAD: British Columbia's economy is dominated by its forest industry, and lumber, wood chips, plywood, pulp, and paper are exported to customers worldwide. A Fraser Estuary barge is pictured here being loaded with wood chips. Photo by Thomas Kitchin/First Light

## Forestry

Chances are good that discussions during most British Columbian's business day will involve some aspect of the forest industry. The forest industry dominates the British Columbia economy. Lumber, wood chips, plywood, pulp, and paper flow in an endless stream to customers around the world.

Evidence of the industry abounds. A visitor flying into Vancouver International Airport will be impressed by the large log booms off Point Grey, where the University of British Columbia is located. He'll also see tugs towing large scows filled with wood chips destined for the province's pulp mills or for export. And, as he walks around Stanley Park, just minutes from the heart of the city's business district, he sees huge ocean freighters from the U.S., Europe, Japan, and Korea with lumber piled high on their decks.

A visitor would not have to venture far outside the Vancouver metropolitan area before seeing fully loaded logging trucks. But he would quickly notice a difference in their cargoes. At the coast the logs are massive—Douglas firs, western red cedar, spruce, hemlock, and cypress—extracted from the dank rain forests. In the interior, which is much drier, the trees are far smaller, spindly lodgepole pine, white pine, and larch, but they stretch oceanlike from horizon to horizon, a resource that has brought prosperity to thousands.

The forest industry has many participants with different skills. The aristocrats (the strongest and toughest) are the fallers (nobody in B.C. calls them lumberjacks), who wield heavy chainsaws to cut down the forest

giants. It's a dangerous occupation to dispatch a Douglas fir weighing many tons when you are unsure of your footing on wet, rough terrain.

In the bush the fallers are joined by others, equally hardy, who trim and buck the trees into truck-size lengths and the chokermen who set the steel cables with which the trees are hauled from the forests. In the interior the smaller trees are literally cut from the forest by mechanical contraptions that look like giant scissors.

At the coast, where the terrain is rough, logging roads have to be carved into mountainsides for access to the forests. A fully loaded logging truck carries a monstrous load, and its driver must navigate frightening switchbacks as he delivers his cargo.

In some areas, where it's impossible to construct a road or where the cost would be prohibitive, heavy-lift helicopters are used to pluck especially high-valued timber off remote mountain bluffs.

Aircraft are also used extensively for protection against fires. At Sproat Lake on Vancouver Island, near

the big MacMillan Bloedel forestry complex at Port Alberni, massive red and white Martin Mars flying boats (the biggest ever operated) swing gently in the breeze, awaiting a call to fight a forest fire. When the call comes, the Mars can be airborne within minutes, passing a scant 150 feet over the treetops to deliver 6,000 gallons of chemically treated water over an area of three to four acres. They reload with water immediately, taking on 30 tons in about 22 seconds as they skim the surface of a lake or inlet at 80 miles an hour. The Mars are owned and operated by a consortium of forest-industry companies.

At Abbotsford Airport in the Fraser Valley, not far from Vancouver, there is the largest private fleet of fire-fighting aircraft in the world, owned and operated by Conair Aviation Ltd. Conair is a British Columbia success story, a commercial operation created to serve the local forest industry, which has spread its wings literally all over the world. Conair's fleet of 50 fixed-wing aircraft includes converted Douglas DC-6Bs (passenger planes from the 1950s) as well as former U.S. Navy reconnaissance aircraft. A subsidiary company operates a fleet of 30 helicopters.

The forest industry has spawned a great body of expertise in the province. There are computer companies that have developed specific software programs to help manage inventories and production processes, and there are consultants who now operate mainly overseas helping in the design and construction of sawmills and pulp mills and the management of forest resources internationally.

British Columbia, which boasts some of the finest softwood forests in the world, accounts for 6 per cent of the world's yearly harvest of softwood trees and 40 per cent of world exports of softwood lumber.

In 1988 British Columbia produced 36.7 million cubic feet of lumber, or 61 per cent of all lumber manufactured in Canada. The province's mills also produced 7 million tonnes of pulp, 30 per cent of the Canadian total, and 2.9 million tonnes of paper, or 17.5 per cent of the national total.

The industry directly employs 86,670 British Columbians in manufacturing and processing facilities located throughout all regions of the province. Annual wages are an estimated $3.3 billion. Indirect employment accounts for an additional 173,330 jobs in B.C. In total, the forest industry is the source of livelihood for 260,000 British Columbians, or close to 20 per cent of the provincial labor force.

In 1988 the industry's shipments were valued at $13.3 billion. Exports accounted for $10.1 billion and forest products used domestically totalled $3.2 billion.

### Tourism

Tourism is second only to forestry in its importance to the British Columbia economy, a fact that shouldn't surprise anyone since few places in the world boast the

scenic attractions or the wealth of outdoor activities that bless Canada's westernmost province.

Visitors can watch for whales off Vancouver Island, fish for salmon in some of the best sports-fishing waters in the world, fly by bush plane to remote hunting and fishing camps, pan for gold in mountain streams, ski, golf, sail, hang-glide, scuba dive, visit the theatre, listen to the symphony, camp in the wilderness, or dine in splendor in big-city restaurants. And everywhere they will want to take photographs—of mountains, flowers, ships, and people.

Expo '86, a 165-day international exposition celebrating travel and communications, which drew about 7 million visitors, is regarded as a watershed in the tourism business in British Columbia. It was intended to raise the province's visibility as a desirable tourist destination, and it was enormously successful.

Many people worried that the province would never be able to equal the revenues of $3.3 billion generated in the Expo year of 1986. They were wrong. The fair (and the province), aptly called "Super, Natural," worked its magic. While tourism revenues dipped to just a little more than $3 billion in 1987, by 1988 they had already reached $3.55 billion, easily surpassing the Expo year.

The industry's present rate of growth is expected to continue into the 1990s, given favorable economic conditions.

FACING PAGE: A fisherman tries his luck at Lake O'Hara in Yoho National Park. A favorite destination for tourists, Yoho is located near the Alberta border along the Continental Divide of the Canadian Rockies. Photo by Al Harvey/Masterfile

ABOVE: A stunning view of Quintet Peaks in the Purcell Mountains prompted some nature lovers to set up camp in this scenic location. Photo by J.A. Kraulis/Masterfile

British Columbia had a total of 19.1 million visitors in 1988, an increase of 14 per cent over 1987 and slightly above the 1986 figure of 18.92 million. About 67 per cent (12.73 million visitors) were travelling for one or more nights, with the remaining 33 per cent or 6.35 million being excursionists (travelling more than 80 kilometres from home but not staying overnight).

British Columbians touring their own province account for more than 50 per cent of overnight visitors, followed by Americans and visitors from other Canadian provinces (mostly neighboring Alberta.) While overseas visitors accounted for only 8 per cent of the overnight stays in 1988, they were big spenders, representing a disproportionate 16.5 per cent of total revenues.

During the winter thousands of British Columbia's visitors enjoy themselves by skiing. The province's hundreds of thousands of square miles of mountainous terrain serve up a magnificent variety of skiing suitable for everyone from the beginner to the most skilled.

The local skiing industry is very well developed, with no fewer than 35 downhill skiing resorts and 29 Nordic skiing destinations, many of them associated with downhill areas. Also there are dozens of provincial parks where skiing is combined with the best outdoor experiences and scenery. B.C. easily qualifies as a skier's paradise.

FACING PAGE: A significant part of British Columbia's tourism industry, skiing is enjoyed by residents and visitors alike. Helicopter skiing is gaining in popularity as depicted by these hardy skiers as they set off down a virgin slope of crystal white powder in the Cariboos. Photo by Alec Pytlowany/ Masterfile

ABOVE: The landmark Empress Hotel in Victoria, a stately reminder of the province's British heritage, has become a stop on the itineraries of many tours. Photo by Thomas Kitchin/Tom Stack & Associates

RIGHT: The British Columbia film industry now provides direct employment for more than 4,000 people and has created a strong market for support services such as food catering, film processing, and post-production. Photo by Gary Fiegehen/First Light

Much effort and money has been invested over the past decade to develop the resort municipality of Whistler, nestled in the mountains about an hour's drive north of Vancouver. It now boasts fine hotels, restaurants, nightclubs, boutiques, golf courses, swimming pools, a convention centre, and a light-hearted holiday ambience. It attracts an international clientele. Lifts, just a few yards apart, take skiers to runs on two mountains: Whistler and Blackcomb.

Helicopter skiing is gaining in popularity, and companies based in Whistler Village provide services to more than 100 other runs on glaciers near the resort.

While there is skiing throughout the province, the most attractive to many visitors are the three resorts situated on the north shore mountains of Vancouver, at Cypress Bowl, Grouse Mountain, and Mount Seymour.

British Columbia attracts many people who like to spice their vacations with a little adventure. The choices include vacations spent on working ranches alongside cowboys, white-water river rafting, viewing big game

animals, scuba diving, mountain climbing, ocean kayaking, and hiking along remote mountain trails. The choices seem endless and are limited only by the visitor's own imagination.

**The Film Industry**
"Lights! Camera! Action!" Throughout British Columbia the movie industry is much in evidence. The province has become a "hot property," and over the last few years Vancouver has grown to become the fifth-largest production centre in North America.

The province's spectacular scenery is responsible for much of this activity. Directors want to shoot in B.C. because of the great variety of locations. But that's not the entire story.

Much of the credit for attracting filmmakers goes to the provincial government, which created the B.C. Film Commission in 1978 to stimulate the industry. The year of its birth, the B.C. film industry was worth $12.5 million. By 1989 more than $200 million was infused into the provincial economy from the shooting of feature films, TV movies, and commercials.

It is estimated that the growing film industry now provides direct employment for more than 4,000 people in the province. Over the years the percentage of local people working on each production has increased from 40 to 97 per cent.

New companies in B.C. now supply the film industry with everything from food catering to film processing, production, and post-production services. Spinoffs benefit restaurants and hotels, vehicle and equipment rental, clothing and cosmetics, interior design, charter services, construction, and many more service industries.

The Film Commission not only promotes the province as a desirable place in which to shoot movies, but it also works closely with film companies, helping them select locations for specific scenes. In addition, it assists producers with budgeting and production scheduling; advises on local crews, technical facilities, and other support services; and acts as a liaison between the production company and the general public, government, and the private sector.

**Mining**
As the decade of the 1990s began, there was excitement in the British Columbia mining industry following the discovery of rich gold and base metal deposits in an area on the remote northern coast that became known as the Golden Triangle. A few small gold discoveries in the area around Stewart started the excitement. Since then several hundred mineral occurrences have been discovered on the surface, and activity has expanded continuously to cover an area of 200 kilometres north to south and 50 kilometres east to west.

Exploration of the mountainous, glacier-covered area is difficult and expensive. The climate is harsh; the snow is wet and heavy; and the exploration season runs only from June to October. Crews and equipment are flown in by fixed-wing aircraft or helicopters. Since there was no suitable access road, one mining company used aircraft to fly out its gold production.

By 1990 more than 250 companies were exploring in the Stewart area looking for gold, copper, lead, zinc, and barite. Sources close to the mining industry estimated that $100 million would be spent on exploration and de-velopment of deposits in the Stewart area in 1990.

As the decade began, mining interests were lobby-ing the British Columbia government for the construc-tion of a road to help further develop the Golden Triangle.

The health of the mining industry depends to a large degree on international economic events beyond its own control. For instance, the demand for coal from British Columbia is related directly to the vigor of the steel in-dustry in Japan. Continued production of gold from some of the higher-cost mines hinges on the world price set on the London Metals Exchange. The price of copper is influenced by production difficulties at mines as far away as Africa and labor disruptions in Peru.

The year 1988 was a record one for the industry. Higher prices, particularly for base metals such as cop-per, zinc, and lead, combined with increased sales vol-umes and continued productivity improvements contributed to a substantial increase in profits. Gross revenues were $3.9 billion, an increase of $714 million over 1987. Industry earnings after taxes were $449 mil-lion, the highest level of net earnings since 1979. Coal was responsible for 41 per cent of the total B.C. mining revenues, and coal shipments represented 92 per cent of the total tonnes shipped.

More than 14,500 people were employed directly in the B.C. mining industry in 1988.

## The Fishing Industry

For many thousands of sports fishermen there are few pleasures as keenly felt and few activities as relaxing as a summer's evening spent in a small boat in sheltered waters along the British Columbia coast as the sun slips toward the western horizon and eager salmon take the bait. Hundreds of charter vessels, from spartan to luxuri-ous, are readily available to cater to visitors of all tastes and budgets.

Commercial fishing, unlike sports fishing, is a major industry in British Columbia but, like all resource indus-tries, it is hostage to the caprice of international com-modity markets, trading arrangements, the relative strength of world currencies, and competition from other fishing fleets.

Some years the fishermen's efforts are rewarded with high prices, while at other times the value of the catch can fall sharply. In 1989, for example, about 304,000 tonnes of fish were harvested by British Columbia's commercial fishermen. The value of the catch was estimated at about $472 million.

British Columbia's harvest accounts for about 35 per cent of the value of the Canadian catch and that includes

virtually all of the salmon and 65 per cent of the herring catch.

Products from British Columbia's fishing grounds meet the demands of customers all over the world.

The waters along the 32,000-kilometre coastline produce a large variety of fish, but by far the most important species are the five varieties of wild Canadian Pacific salmon. While about half of the canned salmon produced in B.C. waters is consumed domestically, almost 90 per cent of the frozen salmon is exported.

The five species of wild Pacific salmon are born in clear streams and migrate to the North Pacific Ocean, where they feed and grow on natural marine nutrients.

The catch is delivered in vessels using modern cooling systems to ensure that it arrives for processing as fresh as possible. The fish are separated by species, size, and grade, and quickly dressed, washed, and packaged for immediate shipment. The West Coast Canadian fishing industry maintains standards that are among the highest in the world. Frozen salmon are first dressed and washed, then flash-frozen and glazed in ice to preserve quality. Just before shipping they are individually protected in plastic bags and packaged in cartons. Black

cod, halibut, groundfish, and shellfish are processed in a similar manner.

Herring roe is especially prized in Japan, where it is considered a delicacy. Japanese demand has had a major impact on the British Columbian fishing industry. Harvested by both purse seine and gillnet, annual roe herring landings range from 15,000 to 60,000 tonnes depending on variations in the stock size and resulting fishing quotas. Upon delivery to the processing plants, the herring is quickly frozen to preserve freshness. Later the herring roe is extracted, cured in brine, graded by size and shape, and shipped to Japan, where it is further processed and marketed under the brand name Kazunokoo.

Other species landed along the British Columbia coast include Black cod, also known as sablefish; Pacific halibut; various species of ground fish (cod, hake, sole, and dog fish); and various shellfish (Dungeness crab, shrimp, prawn, clams, and oysters).

The curious designation "wild" salmon is used to differentiate fish that roam the ocean freely from salmon farmed in pens in sheltered inlets along the coast. Salmon farming is a remarkable success story. Started in Norway, the practice came to British Columbia only recently, but its growth has been dramatic. In 1981 there were only four salmon farms in B.C.; by 1989 there were 135. In less than a decade the value of farmed salmon rose from under one million dollars to an estimated $72 million.

LEFT: The Capilano Salmon Hatchery raises salmon, which are later freed to live in their natural environment. Photo by Edward M. Gifford/ Masterfile

BELOW: About 30,000 people are employed in the fishing industry at the height of the season each year in British Columbia. This Steveston fishing boat returns home after a long day's haul as night descends on the water. Photo by Gordon J. Fisher/First Light

FACING PAGE: British Columbia's fish harvest is about 35 percent of the value of the entire Canadian catch, with wild Pacific salmon maintaining the lead as the province's most important species. Photo by John de Visser/Masterfile

At the height of the fishing season some 29,750 people are employed fully or part-time in the fish harvesting, fish processing, sport-fishing, and aquaculture sectors in British Columbia. The total fishing industry generates about 16,500 direct man years of employment in B.C. and, indirectly, through spending on goods and services, generates the equivalent of an additional 18,500 man years of employment in other industries in British Columbia and elsewhere in Canada.

### Financial Centre

Vancouver has long been recognized as an important financial centre, but its strategic location as Canada's gateway to the Pacific Rim and the booming countries of Southeast Asia give it an extra dimension in the 1990s.

While it is famous for its beauty, Vancouver is also a sophisticated city with the infrastructure to service the needs of the most demanding businesses.

Vancouver's International Financial Centre has been set up to assist companies with a potential interest in establishing international financial offices in the city. The IFC is a non-profit organization under the sponsorship of British Columbia's Ministry of International Business and Immigration.

It can help identify appropriate opportunities in the financial services industry, advise on the interpretation of the law and regulations governing international financial business in B.C., and facilitate contact between non-British Columbian financial firms and the Vancouver financial community as well as with government departments and regulatory authorities.

Legislation passed by the Canadian federal government in Ottawa and the Government of British Columbia permits Canadian and non-Canadian financial institutions with offices in Vancouver to conduct international financial business and allows them to benefit from significant tax and regulatory exemptions.

Eligible financial businesses are exempt from federal income tax on profits earned from non-resident deposit and loan transactions, provincial income tax on profits earned from international financial transactions, and personal provincial income tax for qualifying employees.

One of the key financial institutions in British Columbia is the Vancouver Stock Exchange, which has an international reputation as one of North America's leading exchanges for the raising of risk capital for start-up or junior exploration companies. When the exchange was started in 1907, its primary purpose was to finance mining exploration ventures. Today trading and financing of exploration companies is still the major portion of its business.

In 1989 the exchange traded 3.98 billion shares with about 75 to 80 per cent in resource-exploration companies. Of 195 new listings, 159 or 81 per cent were resource-exploration companies.

In years past the Vancouver Stock Exchange acquired a reputation for lax scrutiny and a willingness to tolerate some of the excesses of the more flagrant stock promoters. In recent years, however, the exchange has tightened its own rules, stepped up its surveillance, and welcomed tougher regulation by the British Columbia government and the province's securities commission. It has taken many important steps to patch up a damaged reputation.

The Vancouver Stock Exchange remains one of the few public markets in North America where infant companies with bright ideas or hot exploration prospects can raise risk capital with a minimum of fuss from investors. Some important recent gold discoveries would not have been made without the risk financing made possible by the VSE.

CHAPTER FOUR

# Where Cultures Meet

by Judith Alldritt McDowell

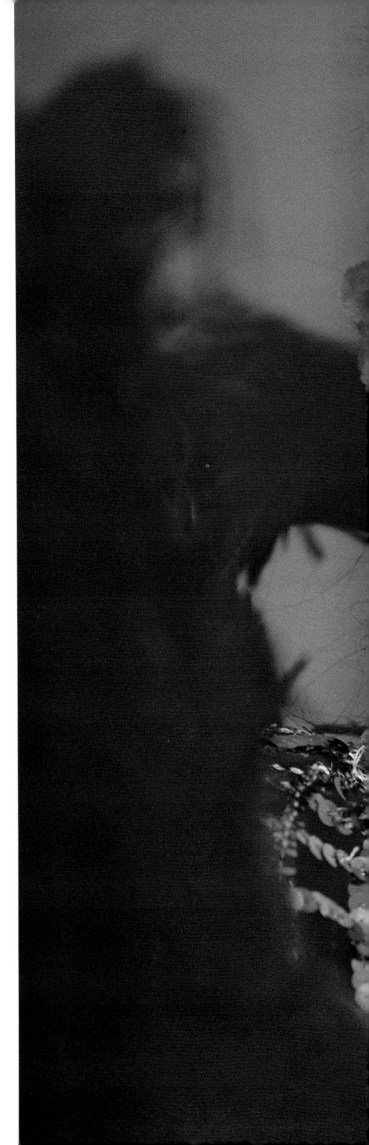

anada owes much of its economic and cultural development in the twentieth century to international immigration, and British Columbia stands out as a place where many cultures meet. Although the province takes its name from the fact that the first European settlers were predominantly citizens of the British Isles, British Columbia society has been shaped throughout its history by the convergence of peoples from a variety of nations and races. Today, as in the past, British Columbians can trace their roots back to many different parts of Canada, North America, and the world.

The vast majority of people living in British Columbia today are relative newcomers. For even the oldest European families, ties in the region go back no more than 50, 100, or 150 years at the most. But for the original inhabitants of this area, ancestral ties to the Pacific Northwest extend back in time for thousands of years. When Spanish and English explorers discovered the region in the eighteenth century, the first people of British Columbia numbered about 70,000 and spoke

A striking young woman of Chinese ancestry participates in a Chinese New Year celebration. The Chinese are the largest group of recent Asian immigrants to settle in British Columbia. Photo by Peter McLeod/First Light

FACING PAGE: A Ksan Indian chief sits before an example of native art in his community of Hazelton. Photo by John de Visser/Masterfile

LEFT: Working meticulously at his craft, a native Haida artisan of the Queen Charlotte Islands creates a new work of art. Photo by J.A. Kraulis/Masterfile

ABOVE: A menacing-looking Kwakiutl totem pole stands over the waters of Queen Charlotte Strait in Alert Bay near the northern tip of Vancouver Island. The Kwakiutl people were among the first inhabitants of the coastal regions of British Columbia, with ancestral ties to the Pacific Northwest that extend back in time for thousands of years. Photo by John de Visser/Masterfile

value as a source of beaver and otter pelts, had no permanent land establishment until 1843. That year the Hudson's Bay Company built a fort and trading post at Victoria. By then the Americans had developed a strong interest in the area, which was part of the vast, largely uncharted Oregon Territory. The conflict that developed between the two powers ended with the Oregon Treaty of 1846, which drew the boundary at the 49th parallel. Three years later, Vancouver Island became a colony of the British empire. The mainland later became a separate colony called British Columbia.

The discovery of gold on the Fraser River in 1858 put British Columbia on the map and started a stampede

10 different groups of languages. Although many groups such as the Coast Salish, the Kwakiutl, and the Bella Coola made their homes near the water, where the weather was mild, the food plentiful, and transportation easy, others such as the Tsimshian, the Dene, and the Kootenay inhabited the mountains and river valleys of the northwest, the northern interior, and the southeastern corner of the province.

British and Spanish sailors may have passed through the area in the sixteenth century, but their first recorded visits occurred in the 1790s when Spain and England were both intent on finding the fabled Northwest Passage. A clash was avoided when, in 1792, Captain George Vancouver met with the Spanish at Nootka Sound on the west coast of Vancouver Island and struck a deal that gave the British undisputed access to the waters of the Pacific Northwest.

The British, who wanted rights in the region because of its

of American prospectors from California, many of whom stayed on to homestead. Among the 30,000 gold seekers were 1,000 Chinese merchants and several groups of free American blacks who were fleeing discriminatory laws in California. Encouraged by 160-acre land grants from the British government, more and more immigrants started arriving during the 1860s.

Less than a century after the first contact with Europeans, the rich native culture of the Pacific Northwest had been destroyed by the combined influences of alcohol, gunpowder, disease, and the power of government, which gave away the aboriginals' land and outlawed

their rituals. By the end of the nineteenth century, with their culture broken and their population reduced to a few thousand, the aboriginals of the region had either left their increasingly empty villages for the new city of Vancouver or had been forced onto reservations.

Although farming, fishing, mining, logging, and sawmilling were all established in the region by the 1860s, settlement remained slow until the 1880s, when the Canadian Pacific Railway built a line from central Canada to the coast. In the meantime, the two separate colonies of British Columbia and Vancouver Island had amalgamated (1866). In 1871 British Columbia agreed to join the Dominion of Canada, a newly formed confederation of the British colonies in North America. One condition of joining was the promise of a railway.

At that time the total population of British Columbia consisted of about 11,000 immigrants and 30,000 aboriginals. Victoria was the largest town, with 4,000 inhabitants. Vancouver did not exist yet, but 1,000 immigrants had settled in New Westminister on the Fraser River. A few thousand miners remained in Barkerville, and others were scattered through the former gold fields in the Cariboo and the Fraser Canyon. Some homesteaders, including a number of black immigrants, had moved into the Gulf Islands, the Fraser Valley, and the arable river valleys of the interior.

The railway took six years to build (May 1880 to May 1886), and when it was finished, British Columbia

BELOW: The popular Victoria Day Parade, pictured here, celebrates the official birthday of Queen Victoria on May 1 of each year. Photo by Brian Milne/First Light

FACING PAGE: A host of events and festivals helps to celebrate the diverse ethnic history of the British Columbia people. A crew of more than 20 women are shown here as they propel their dragonboat through the water in a race off the Vancouver shoreline. Photo by Dave Watters/First Light

began to boom. The railway brought new people to the province by the thousands, and most of them brought energy, ideas, and ambition. Unfortunately, some of them also brought greed, cunning, and racial prejudice.

Fifteen thousand Chinese, Japanese, and South Asian indentured workers had been imported to build the railway, and although many later returned home, others stayed in B.C. They often worked in the early forest industry or as house servants for a growing class of wealthy entrepreneurs. Shunned and hated by the whites of that period, Asians lived, ate, and shopped within their own communities. In Vancouver a Japantown and a large Chinatown sprang up on the mudflats bordering False Creek. Victoria and other B.C. towns also had sizable Asian populations. However, because of restrictions on Asian immigration, which included a $500 head tax, 90 per cent of the orientals in B.C. were male until the 1940s.

Many of the Asian immigrants stayed, worked hard, opened businesses, sent money home, and looked after themselves. The Japanese became intensely involved in the fishing and canning industry, and the Chinese and Japanese both developed stakes in the agricultural sector as vegetable growers.

Today some of the wealthiest business interests in the province are Chinese, and the area around Pender Street in Vancouver's Chinatown contains some of the most valuable real estate in the city.

The end of the nineteenth century was a turbulent boom time of rapid development in which the population of Vancouver soared from a few hundred in the 1870s to 27,000 in 1900. Ten years later it had nearly quadrupled, reaching 100,000 by 1911. By 1914, at the outbreak of World War I, the province as a whole had reached a total population of 400,000. Most of this increase was accounted for by immigrants, 90 per cent of whom were English-speaking—mostly either Canadian-born migrants from the eastern provinces or British citizens from Commonwealth countries (England, Wales, Scotland, Ireland, Australia, New Zealand, and South Africa). Several thousand came from the United States, and from Europe came a number of Germans, Scandinavians, Russians, and Italians. Asian immigration nearly disappeared during these years.

Of course, not all of the newcomers to B.C. headed for the coast. Some were looking for gold and silver, and some wanted land on which to ranch and raise their families. Traveling overland by horse-drawn wagon or by riverboat and, later, by rail, immigrants found gold, silver, and land in the Fraser Valley, the Cariboo region, and among the peaks and valleys of the Kootenays in southwestern B.C. Ranchers discovered the Okanagan early on, and British orchardists later put down roots there and on Vancouver Island.

A few settlers even found their way to the frozen north in search of arable valleys and unlimited range land. Until the coming of the railways, land was incredibly cheap almost everywhere in the interior.

In 1910 the building of the Grand Trunk Pacific Railway from Prince George near Yellowhead Pass to Prince Rupert on the north coast created a northern land boom similar to the ones in the southeast.

During these early years, the British influence

ABOVE: Loggers thrive on danger, and each summer during the All Sooke Days festival men race to the top of towering trees with only a safety belt for protection. Photo by Freeman Patterson/ Masterfile

RIGHT: This attention-grabbing mural depicting the community's heritage adorns the wall of Nelson's local museum. Almost every city and town in British Columbia features a museum dedicated to local history and pioneer life. Photo by Thomas Kitchin/ First Light

dominated life in British Columbia. This expressed itself in the politics of the province, which were conservative, and popular sentiment, which was Royalist. But the loyalty of British Columbians to "the old country" showed most strongly in World War I. A full 10 per cent of the male population (43,000 men) served overseas. Half of them either died or came back wounded.

When the war ended in 1918, British Columbia had been settled for more than 60 years, and it seemed as though the boom years were over forever. Soldiers returned home to find that they couldn't get a job. But in

B.C. the economic stagnation was only temporary. By the early 1920s the economic outlook had brightened, and the years before the Depression were increasingly prosperous.

If the end of the war caused temporary stagnation in British Columbia, Europe was in an even worse state, and people were only too glad to leave if they had the chance. Northern Europeans (Germans, Scandanavians, Netherlanders) began making their way to Canada in larger numbers in the early 1920s, though both immigrant and native-born populations in British Columbia

remained overwhelmingly British in origin. Despite being classified by the immigration policy of the time as "non-preferred," immigrants from southern, central, and eastern Europe also increased during this period. The biggest numerical increase originated in eastern Europe. Spurred by famine and political repression at home, Russian and Ukrainian immigration reached a new high in the late 1920s.

When the Depression hit, immigration from Europe all but ceased as Canadians sought to protect the jobs that were left by restricting entry to the country. Asian

The Second World War, in which the people of B.C. again displayed their loyalty to Britain, brought an end to the Depression. All British Columbians suffered as a result of the war, but the Japanese Canadians endured a special kind of personal and economic agony. Anyone of Japanese origin, no matter how long he or his family had resided in B.C., was rounded up and had his land and other assets confiscated. Even worse, whole families were either imprisoned in central B.C. or deported to Japan. Only in 1990 did the government of Canada publicly acknowledge its error in treating citizens of Japanese extraction as enemies of the state and agree to make a cash reparation payment to survivors.

The postwar years were a time of rapid growth in all B.C.'s basic industries, including the new economic stars—natural gas and hydro-electric power, and the province's population was growing again as people came from all over Canada and the world to share in B.C.'s increasing prosperity. Migration from within Canada has been a significant factor in the province's population growth throughout its history, but the high point of international immigration occurred during the 20 years from 1945 to 1965, when so-called "displaced persons" and refugees from the war in Europe swelled the numbers of immigrants.

This was also the beginning of a shift in the traditional balance between British (English-speaking) and European immigration. From this point on, non-English-speaking immigrants would become more visible, and the British influence would gradually recede in importance. In the years following the war, as British Columbia absorbed more and more Poles, Hungarians,

ABOVE: Vancouver's Sea Fest is one of numerous local fairs and exhibitions held in British Columbia throughout the summer and autumn. Here, some tasty fish is being prepared for the hungry crowd. Photo by Edward M. Gifford/Masterfile

FACING PAGE: With style, sophistication, and a zest for life, British Columbians are proud of their unique and diverse heritage. Photo by Robert Semeniuk/ First Light

BELOW RIGHT: A new wave of immigration after World War II altered the face of traditional British Columbia society. Eastern Europeans, Asians, Americans, and Indians discovered the benefits of the province and flowed into the region in search of a new life. The largest group of recent Asian immigrants are Chinese, with Indians qualifying as the second-largest number of immigrants in British Columbia today. Photo by Jim Russell/First Light

immigration was practically nonexistent, anyway, having been tightly controlled since the 1880s.

During the Depression, British Columbians suffered from the collapse in the world demand for the province's major products: non-ferrous metals, lumber, fish, beef, and apples and other soft fruit. The agricultural depression on the Canadian prairies forced thousands of people off the land and into the cities. A great many of them ended up in the towns along the B.C. coast.

Czechoslovakians, Greeks, Russians, Italians, and Armenians, the multicultural fabric of the province began to take shape.

Some postwar immigrants came from farms and villages in Europe, but most were from the skilled, urban working class. Many were well-educated, middle-class entrepreneurs and professionals whose lives had been disrupted beyond repair by the war. But no matter what their backgrounds had been, in British Columbia they found the space and freedom that many parts of Europe lacked and an expanding economy in which their talents and energy could thrive.

One example of this kind of postwar immigration was the Dutch dairy farmers who settled in the Fraser Valley in the late 1940s. The descendants of these and earlier Dutch immigrants in B.C. now number more than 70,000, forming one of the largest, and, ironically, least visible, ethnic strains in the province.

In the second half of the twentieth century, the face of British Columbia society has been changed by new waves of immigration—from Europe in the years immediately after the Second World War and from Britain and eastern Europe in the 1950s. Although U.S. immigrants have always played a substantial role in British Columbia society, the anti-Vietnam War movement brought a new generation of young, middle-class Americans to the West Coast in the late 1960s and early 1970s. After long-standing restrictions against Asians were removed in the early 1960s, immigration from Asia gained unprecedented momentum. In 1988, for example, nearly seven out of 10 immigrants to B.C. came from Pacific Rim countries, compared to two out of 10 in 1968. The largest number of recent Asian immigrants are Chinese, and the second most numerous group is from India.

The 1980s have also seen a noticeable increase in immigration from Latin America, much of it the result of political refugees fleeing military repression. Since many Latin American refugees come from the entrepreneurial middle classes, this stream of immigration has introduced a new and dynamic element to business in B.C.

In the late 1980s British Columbia began attracting a

new category of refugees. Under Canada's "investor immigrant" program, Hong Kong residents have invested hundreds of millions of dollars in B.C., the province of first choice for these wealthy refugees from the imminent mainland Chinese takeover of Hong Kong.

As usual, the impact of immigration is most dramatic in the urban centres of the southwest. In Vancouver during the late 1980s one out of every two schoolchildren came from a non-English speaking home. At any one time, 20 per cent of Vancouver students were studying English as a second language.

Nevertheless, after more than a century of growth and change, B.C.'s population is still predominantly British and northern European in origin. But the numerical dominance of these groups diminishes with every succeeding decade. More and more, the people of British Columbia constitute a rich ethnic mix that reflects the diverse and dynamic world outside their borders.

CHAPTER FIVE

# A Fine Place to Live

by Judith Alldritt McDowell

E very year thousands of people decide to move to British Columbia for a variety of reasons. Whether they are looking for a milder climate, a better education, a more satisfying job, cleaner air and water, or a chance to live, work, and play in one of the most beautiful natural settings in the world, people who choose British Columbia for their home rarely feel they have made a mistake. And for natives of the province, leaving is often out of the question, no matter what other parts of the world may offer.

Among British Columbia's attractions are its educational opportunities and high standard of health and social services. Then there is its sensitive justice system and democratic system of government, opportunities for self-expression in the fields of art and entertainment, a wide range of modern indoor leisure facilities, and a landscape in which most forms of outdoor recreation just seem to come naturally.

### Education
The public school system in B.C. consists of more than 1,600 elementary, junior secondary,

With a full-time enrollment of about 8,700 (in 1989), Simon Fraser is British Columbia's second-largest university. It is located on top of Burnaby Mountain on the east side of Vancouver. Photo by Ed Gifford/Masterfile

FACING PAGE: More than 1,100 public elementary schools serve the educational needs of British Columbia towns from small communities such as Good Hope Lake shown here to the larger cities of Prince George, Kamloops, and Kelowna. Photo by Barry Dursley/First Light

RIGHT: Sometimes education steps outside of the traditional classroom in an effort to introduce children to all facets of the learning process. Some young Vancouver artists-in-training are pictured here as they receive instruction in sketching at a local museum. Photo by Chuck O'Rear/First Light

BELOW: In this Chinese public school in Victoria, students learn to write in the language of their ancestors. British Columbia's public school system consists of about 1,600 elementary, junior secondary, and senior secondary schools. Photo by Brian Milne/First Light

and senior secondary schools covering kindergarten through grade 12. Schools are supported financially by a combination of municipal property taxes and funds taken from the general revenues of the provincial government. B.C. also has a well-developed system of more than 200 independent, fee-based schools, some religious and some secular, at both the elementary and secondary levels. More than 32,000 students were enroled in this system in 1990. Independent schools are eligible for education grants from the provincial government based on the number of students attending. In 1990 these grants amounted to more than $45 million.

Attendance at either a public school, a recognized independent school, or other satisfactory alternative is compulsory for children between the ages of seven and 15. Thanks to B.C.'s system of free school bus transportation, students in rural areas can attend classes at fully equipped schools in semi-rural and urban centres.

The provincial Ministry of Education also operates a complete correspondence school program for elementary and secondary school students who for reasons of distance or disability cannot attend classes in person. Beginning in early September and ending in late June, the school year lasts about 39 weeks with a break for Christmas and another spring break about halfway between Christmas and the end of June.

Public schools in B.C. offer training and education in a wide assortment of fields both technical and academic, from English and geometry to automotive repair and theatre arts. The curriculum is revised periodically to make sure that the system remains up-to-date and capable of meeting the needs of contemporary students. The most recent major overhaul of the system occurred in 1989 with the drafting of a new *Schools Act* based on the findings of a Royal Commission on Education, which toured the province seeking advice from all sectors of the community. The purpose of the new system is to develop citizens who are, among other things, thoughtful and able to think critically; creative, flexible, and self-motivated; capable of making independent decisions; skilled; productive; cooperative, principled, and respectful of others; and prepared to exercise the rights of an individual within the family, the community, Canada, and the world.

Teachers in B.C. schools must meet high standards of qualifications, and competition for positions is intense because of the comfortable climate and the many other attractive features of life in Canada's westernmost province. B.C.'s young people reap the benefit of this competition in the form of a large stock of well-qualified teachers.

At the post-secondary level, B.C.'s 22 colleges, institutes, and universities serve a total of about 135,000 students each year. The province has three institutes—the

B.C. Institute of Technology, the Emily Carr College of Art, and the Pacific Marine Training Institute—and three universities, of which the oldest is the University of British Columbia (UBC) in Vancouver with approximately 27,000 students. Located at the tip of Point Grey peninsula on the bluffs overlooking the Strait of Georgia and Burrard Inlet, UBC occupies a spectacular site; and its facilities are no less advantageous than its location. With first-rate professional schools in law, medicine, and architecture, UBC is also well known for its achievements in scientific disciplines such as forestry, engineering, physics, computer science, and chemistry and for the high quality and dedication of its arts, humanities, and social science faculties.

UBC is also the home of TRIUMF, Canada's national laboratory for subatomic research. TRIUMF (the name stands for tri-university meson facility) houses the largest and most complex cyclotron in the world, one of only three such machines in existence. The cyclotron is a high-speed particle accelerator that emits a high-intensity proton beam used in medical, industrial, commercial, and scientific applications. Each year TRIUMF projects involve 100 or more graduate students from four different universities.

The University of Victoria, located in the provincial capital, and Simon Fraser University, located on top of Burnaby Mountain on the east side of Vancouver, both date from the early 1960s. Although less than half the

size of UBC, Victoria and Simon Fraser offer a high standard of instruction in the full range of academic disciplines. Their size makes these two smaller universities the first choice for many students and faculty who prefer a more intimate campus atmosphere.

More facilities for higher education are on the drawing board. The Ministry of Advanced Education and Job Training has embarked on a major expansion program that will, by 1995, create room for 15,000 additional university students; convey full degree-granting rights to colleges in Kelowna, Kamloops, and Nanaimo; create a new university in northern B.C.; and increase access to post-secondary education for native people and the disabled.

All three B.C. universities maintain a lively relationship with their local communities through cultural events such as art exhibitions, theatre, and concerts and through community education programs in a wide variety of popular subject areas from language studies to business management. Simon Fraser University has developed a special approach to community outreach by

opening a downtown campus in the heart of Vancouver's business and shopping district.

Educational institutions in B.C. are in the forefront of developments in distance education, a form of outreach that uses satellite television, computers, and other kinds of technology to bring learning opportunities to students in remote locations. Total enrolment in distance education courses in B.C. is nearly 70,000. B.C. also participates in a number of international education programs, many of which involve a distance education component. Delegates to the 1987 Commonwealth Conference in Vancouver were so impressed with the potential of the distance education technology developed here that they formed "The Commonwealth of Learning," an international organization based in Vancouver and dedicated to developing distance education programs in Commonwealth countries.

At home in B.C., the Open Learning Agency in Vancouver reaches out to the world of adult learners through television, providing more than 850 credit and non-credit courses presented on the cable channel known as the Knowledge Network. Established in 1982 and linked to colleges and universities throughout the province that supply the courses and faculty, the Open Learning Agency helps thousands of British Columbians each year to achieve professional development goals or to qualify for university entrance.

In addition to the three universities in Vancouver and Victoria, British Columbia has an extensive network of 15 trade, technical, and community colleges with more than 100 branches in different communities around the province. The college system offers post-secondary training across a broad educational front, from university-entry academic programs to cooking and heavy machinery repair. Although most colleges are located in the heavily populated areas of the lower mainland and southern Vancouver Island, vocational and college-entry programs are also available in Nanaimo and Comox on Vancouver Island and in several interior communities such as Prince George, Nelson, Castlegar, Kelowna, and Dawson Creek.

## Health Care

In British Columbia health is viewed as "a resource for living," and health care is considered a basic right of every resident regardless of age or economic status. All British Columbians benefit from a system of universal medical insurance that is funded by a combination of

ABOVE: British Columbia boasts an extensive network of 15 trade, technical, and community colleges with more than 100 branches throughout the province in addition to the three main universities in Vancouver and Victoria. The province's educational institutions are also at the forefront of developments in distance education. Photo by Thomas Bruckbauer/ First Light

LEFT: Medical research goes hand in hand with quality health care, and British Columbia's specialized clinics are staffed by medical researchers dedicated to finding new ways of treating common health problems. Photo by John D. Luke/First Light

FACING PAGE: The University of British Columbia (UBC) in Vancouver, the province's largest university, sits atop the bluffs of the Point Grey peninsula overlooking the Strait of Georgia and Burrard Inlet. Among the school's offerings are its first-rate professional schools in law, medicine, and architecture. Photo by J.A. Kraulis/Masterfile

ABOVE: The provincial legislature, which is known as the Legislative Assembly, meets in the nineteenth-century stone and stained-glass Parliament Buildings overlooking Victoria's Inner Harbor. Photo by Bob Herger/First Light

FACING PAGE: The simple, modern lines of the courthouse in Vancouver contrast greatly with the ornate, nineteenth-century architecture of the Parliament Buildings in Victoria. The provincial judiciary system includes the Court of Appeal, the Supreme Court of B.C., the county courts, and the provincial courts. Photo by Al Harvey/Masterfile

employer/employee-paid premiums and general tax revenues. People with incomes below a certain level pay only a nominal premium but receive the same quality of care as anyone else. Physicians bill the medical insurance plan directly according to an agreed schedule of fees for particular services. Hospitals receive an annual operating grant from the provincial government that covers staff and equipment costs.

The quality of medical care provided under the B.C. health system is on a par with the most advanced medical care anywhere in the world. Major hospitals in the larger metropolitan areas are fully equipped with the latest diagnostic, treatment, and monitoring equipment. Examples include the cell separator used in preparing special blood transfusions for leukemia patients and the magnetic resonance imaging (MRI) diagnostic unit recently installed at a cost of more than $4 million at Vancouver General Hospital.

For British Columbians living at a distance from a major metropolitan hospital, the province operates an extensive ground, sea, and air ambulance service that is always available to transfer patients from local clinics to an appropriately equipped medical facility. For hard-to-treat health issues such as insomnia, chronic pain, and eating disorders, a variety of special clinics are staffed by medical researchers dedicated to finding new ways of treating common problems. Mental health services include free psychiatric counselling and a network of community clinics, boarding homes, and hospitals for people who require intensive care. To complete the picture, B.C.'s health care system also supports an energetic, province-wide public health program, an up-to-date program of disease control and prevention, comprehensive in-home care services for the elderly and disabled, and a large network of long-term care hospitals for the chronically ill.

## Government and Justice

Under the Canadian constitution, health, education, and other social services are the responsibility of the provincial government, and the degree of public support for these services is always a topic of heated political debate in the provincial legislature. Officially named the Legislative Assembly, the provincial legislature is unicameral, and the Members of the Legislative Assembly, known as MLAs, are elected to represent geographical areas known as ridings.

The form of government in B.C. comes from the British system in which the elected leader of the majority party is also the Premier or chief executive officer of the government. The executive functions of the government are managed by the Executive Council, whose members are chosen by the Premier from among the leading members of the majority party in the legislature.

The Legislative Assembly is made up of 69 MLAs who meet for several weeks each year in the provincial Parliament Buildings, a splendid nineteenth-century stone-and-stained-glass structure overlooking the inner harbor in Victoria. The MLAs are all elected at the same time and serve for a maximum of five years, although the government seldom lasts for a full five-year term. Under the parliamentary system, the party in power can call another election at any time, and it rarely waits until the clock runs out, preferring to pick a moment when the mood of the electorate is favorable. The election usually comes during a period when economic conditions are good and people are relatively happy with the governing party.

British Columbia has several political parties, but only two—the Social Credit Party and the New Democratic Party—have held power since the 1950s. The New Democrats held power from 1972 to 1975. For the balance of the last 40 years, the Social Credit Party has governed the province, with the New Democratic Party (NDP) as the official opposition. The Liberal and Conservative parties, though powerful in other provinces and at the level of national politics, have lost most of their members in B.C. to Social Credit, which refers to itself as the "private enterprise party" because of its declared allegiance to the interests of business. In contrast, the NDP has strong ties to the labor unions and might be called the "social enterprise party" because of its support for policies that serve the working class and the underprivileged.

British Columbia has two separate court systems—federal and provincial—and all judges are appointed by the government in power. Provincial courts enforce laws dealing with civil and property rights inside B.C. Criminal cases are heard in the federal courts and come under the Criminal Code of Canada. The Supreme Court of Canada is the highest court in the country and hears appeals from higher courts at both the federal and provincial levels, including cases that arise from the Canadian bill of rights, called the Charter of Rights and Freedoms.

Though elected by local residents, municipal governments get their authority from the provincial legislature, which also shares in the cost of some municipal services and capital projects. The vast majority of the money needed to run towns and cities comes from property taxes, however. Cities, towns, and villages look after services such as garbage collection, police and fire protection, social housing, and water supply. Recreation facilities such as sports arenas, swimming pools, and local parks also fall under municipal jurisdiction.

Often it is more efficient for several municipalities in the same region to share responsibility for some of these functions. The job of administering shared functions falls to another level of government, the regional district, as in

The Law Courts

**ABOVE: A pack of windsurfers utilize both muscle power and skill to manoeuvre their sailboards off the Vancouver waterfront. Photo by Al Harvey/Masterfile**

**RIGHT: Fly fishing can be a peaceful way to spend a day as this fisherman discovered in the wilderness north of Kamloops. Photo Al Harvey/Masterfile**

the Greater Vancouver Regional District or the Capital Regional District, which serves Victoria. A relatively recent addition to the political fabric in British Columbia, regional districts get their money from municipal and provincial grants. Their instrument of government is a board made up of elected representatives from the participating municipalities.

## Parks and Recreation

So far we have been talking about some essential elements in the life of any community—education, health care, and government. British Columbians take pride in looking after the basics, but most would agree that there is a lot more to life than that. In fact, if British Columbians come together on anything, it would be on the absolute importance of having a good time.

An appreciation of the natural environment is practically a requirement for residence in British Columbia, where it seems that every conceivable form of outdoor recreation has its own large group of devoted followers. Whether it is skiing, trail bike riding, kayaking, whitewater rafting, fishing, sailing, camping, hiking, hanggliding, bird watching, or golf—you name it—in B.C. there is a time and a place and a reason for doing it. Sometimes the reason is simply the fact that it's there—"it" being the mountain, the lake, the ocean, the

beach, the river, or the trail. Because whatever it takes in the way of natural landscape, public parks, and indoor or outdoor recreation facilities to make a people healthy and happy, British Columbia has it all.

Numbers never tell the whole story, of course, but in this case anyone would have to admit they're impressive. Contemplate, for instance, what B.C.'s 41,000 kilometres of intricate coastline mean to pleasure boaters, marine kayakers, sports fishermen, and beachcombers—more magnificent, undiscovered territory than the most fanatical weekend explorer could ever hope to exhaust in a lifetime. No wonder British Columbia has more than 200 private marinas and more pleasure boats per capita than any other province in Canada. And, with

dozens of salmon rivers emptying into the ocean, it is no wonder that British Columbia issues nearly 300,000 tidewater fishing licenses every year. Add to that the 30 marine parks the provincial government maintains on the coast, and it's obvious that boating is a big part of the meaning in life for the 60 per cent of British Columbians who live within a wave's roar of the ocean.

Some of the same people—many of them whole families—who live to go sailing in summer are just as enthusiastic about skiing in winter. In a landscape dominated by steep, snow-capped mountains, it isn't surprising that skiing is becoming almost as important to the B.C. way of life as water sports. With a choice of 35 downhill and 29 Nordic ski areas, including internation-

ally known resorts such as Whistler, scattered through every region of the province, plus dozens of provincial parks where it is possible to ski surrounded by spectacular scenery, British Columbians have both motive and opportunity for becoming demon skiers. And for the high-flying, adventurous skiers who can be satisfied with nothing less than the total scenic and physical exhilaration of a run down a glacier, there is the excitement of heliskiing.

Though skiing and sailing have big followings, they are only part of the picture. Camping, hiking, and other down-to-earth ways of enjoying the out of doors are such a large part of life in British Columbia that it sometimes seems as though the whole province is one big

park, and in a way that is true. More than 90 per cent of the land in B.C. is publicly owned, and over 80 per cent is forested. These facts have helped British Columbians create an enviable system of public parks that includes (at last count) 390 separate provincial parks and recreation areas with 11,300 campsites, 5,000 picnic tables, 115 boat-launching ramps, 66,500 metres of developed beaches, and 2,000 kilometres of maintained trails. Covering a total area of more than 5.4 million hectares or one-twentieth of the province, British Columbia's parklands are bigger than all of Switzerland. Provincial parks range in size from less than a

hectare to nearly 900,000 hectares in Tweedsmuir Provincial Park in the Coast Mountain Range, and one out of 10 is a wilderness area.

In addition to the provincial parks, there are four national parks in British Columbia, all located in some of the most magnificent, pristine landscape in North America, and hundreds of fine city and regional parks. A good example is the ring of parks in and around Victoria that is operated by the Capital Regional District. A prize city park known all over the world is Vancouver's own pride and joy, Stanley Park, a unique semi-wilderness located in the heart of one of the world's most dense population centres. Rivaling Stanley Park in size and significance is the new Pacific Spirit Park, which was recently created out of the large tracts of undeveloped

land adjacent to the University of British Columbia. Reputed to be the world's largest urban park, Pacific Spirit covers 2,100 acres of mostly untouched first-growth rain forest, penetrated only by pedestrian pathways.

While it is easy to extoll the pleasures of the natural environment in British Columbia, it is important not to overlook how well equipped most communities are with indoor recreation facilities. The winter theme carries through year round in indoor skating rinks, which are often a home away from home for budding young figure skaters and hockey stars. Evenings and weekends probably find parents and other relatives enjoying a turn round the skating rink or flailing at the ice with a broom in that peculiar and all-Canadian team sport known as curling. Though some ice rinks stand alone, they are

often just one part of a community recreation complex that includes a swimming pool, water slide, tennis bubble, weight room, sauna, and spa, and, in at least one case, the Oak Bay Recreation Centre in Victoria, a computer room equipped with educational programs and all the latest computer games.

For the most part these are all publicly supported facilities, and they exist alongside a host of privately owned spas and fitness clubs that have proliferated in the past 15 years to meet the demands of a highly health-conscious population. In fact, one of the more gratifying aspects of residence in British Columbia is the role that both provincial and municipal governments play in supporting public recreation and amateur sport. The government of B.C., for example, distributes more than $12 million a year in grants to physical fitness and amateur sports organizations.

In the midst of all this activity, people in B.C. still have time to enjoy spectator sports. Just witness the fans of professional football and hockey who follow the fortunes of the B.C. Lions or the Vancouver Canucks or the baseball fans who turn out all spring and summer to cheer the Vancouver Canadians. Add to that semi-professional soccer, professional horse racing at Exhibition Park in Vancouver and Sandown Park in Victoria, sports-car and stock-car racing, air shows, and a slew of rip-roaring rodeos in towns all around the province, and you begin to see why British Columbians have a reputation as a sporting crowd.

ABOVE: British Columbia hikers pause to absorb the spectacular scenery from a ridge in the Bugaboos. Photo by Ron Watts/First Light

FACING PAGE BOTTOM: For high-flying skiers who must experience total physical exhilaration of a run down a glacier, there is the thrill of heliskiing. This skier tackles the Cariboos. Photo by Patrick Morrow/First Light

FACING PAGE TOP: British Columbia boasts more than 5 million hectares of parklands, some 2,000 kilometres of maintained trails, and 66,500 metres of developed beaches. And of all the outdoor recreational possibilities that the province offers, water sports seem to be the most popular. Photo by Thomas Bruckbauer/First Light

BELOW: Talented musicians entertain the crowds at the Vancouver Folk Music Festival, an annual open-air jamboree. Photo by Al Harvey/Masterfile

FACING PAGE TOP: A saxophone player emits a melodious tune as evening falls over Vancouver's Sea Fest. Photo by Ross Stojko/Masterfile

FACING PAGE BOTTOM: A troupe of actors in Elizabethan costume takes centre stage in Vancouver's Stanley Park. Photo by J.A. Kraulis/Masterfile

## Art and Entertainment

British Columbians get a little annoyed when their cousins from central Canada imply that B.C. is still a frontier for entertainment and the arts. In this case frontier means a place where new and exciting things are happening.

No matter where you live in B.C., something is always going on—very often a festival celebrating the arts, music, or local folkways. If it's spring in Victoria, for instance, you wouldn't want to miss the annual TerrifVic Jazz Party, a week-long series of indoor and outdoor concerts and events featuring local favorites and jazz giants from around the world. And summer wouldn't be summer in the capital without the traditional festivities that go on behind the Tweed Curtain at the Oak Bay Tea Party on Willows Beach; the expert

other times during the summer and fall, Vancouver hosts such popular cultural events as the New Play Festival, the Fringe Theatre Festival, and the International Film Festival.

For indoor fun there is theatre, opera, ballet, and symphony as well as pop concerts, jazz clubs, museums, and art exhibitions. There is so much to see and do and never enough time to do it all.

Vancouver now ranks as a world centre for performing arts, both as a showcase for B.C. talent and as an essential stop for every conceivable kind of international touring com-

logrolling at the annual logger sports competition during All Sooke Days, or the creative rivalry at the Moss Street Paint-In. The end of summer is marked by the colorful and nostalgic Classic Boat Festival in the Inner Harbor, where you can get your hands on the wheel of a genuine square-rigged schooner and be transported backwards in time.

In the Cariboo-Chilcotin every summer brings displays of hard riding and roping at rodeos such as the Williams Lake Stampede and the Anaheim Lake Stampede, but summer in cowboy country is also the time to celebrate the heritage of the gold rush at historical festivals such as Lillooet Days and Billy Barker Days in Quesnel. Up in the high country beyond the Coast Range, the summer air is filled with the sound of banjos during annual bluegrass festivals at Shuswap and Kamloops. Equally festive in different ways are the annual Squilax Indian Pow Wow, the craft fair at Keremeos, the Cherry Fiesta at Osoyoos, the B.C. Square Dance Jamboree at Penticton, the Old Time Accordian Championship at Kimberley, the Northern Artists' Festival in Prince George, and the B.C. Festival of the Arts, a gala celebration of community visual and performing arts hosted by a different B.C. city or town each year.

Back at the coast, summertime sometimes seems to be one big party. The most exciting time for kids is in May, when the Vancouver Children's Festival attracts dozens of children's entertainers from all over the world for a week of non-stop music, theatre, storytelling, and merrymaking. The adults' turn comes in June with the Du Maurier International Jazz Festival and, again, in July with the incomparable Vancouver Folk Music Festival, an annual open-air jamboree of monumental proportions and an album full of memorable moments. At

pany, from the Joffrey Ballet and *Phantom of the Opera* to the Rolling Stones and the Red Army Chorus. On any night of the week, in any week of the year, it's possible to choose from dozens of events in theatres and nightclubs around the city. And there is plenty of local talent to pick from as well. These days the art and entertainment scene in B.C is bristling with energy and excitement, and resident theatre and dance companies are proliferating at a pace that makes it almost impossible to keep track of it all. New companies such as Ballet B.C. seem to do well right from the start, while established institutions such as the Vancouver Symphony, the Vancouver Playhouse Theatre, the Vancouver Chamber Orchestra, and the Vancouver Art Gallery keep delighting and surprising their loyal audiences.

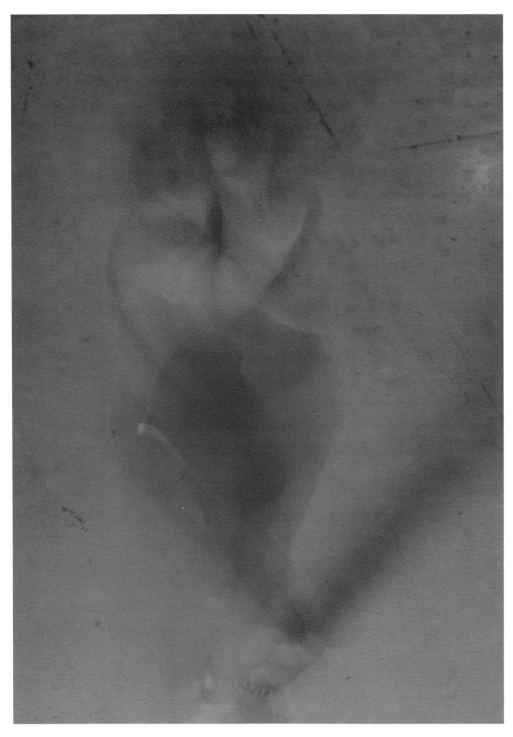

such as the Victoria Symphony, the Pacific Opera, the Victoria Art Gallery, the Belfry Theatre, and Kaleidoscope Children's Theatre as well as fresh, new arts enterprises such as the Victoria Arts Collaborative and Kidco, a touring dance company made up of talented adolescents. In addition, Victoria's McPherson Playhouse and the recently renovated Royal Theatre both host a year-round series of concerts and shows by headliners from all over the world.

But life in British Columbia isn't all lights, music, and action. In fact, the quieter kinds of cultural pursuits, such as reading, are probably the most popular. British Columbians are great readers, and the local publishing industry is one of the liveliest on the continent. B.C. is a paradise for writers, and you don't have to look far to find them. No matter how large or small the town, there is likely to be a poet, a novelist, or an historian on every block.

Making a record of the changing dimensions of life in B.C. is one of the jobs writers and historians do. And making sure that record is available to succeeding generations is the job of museums, libraries, and other public and private storehouses of historical information. B.C. is justly proud of its museum system, which includes hundreds of museums and historic sites lo-

But Vancouverites don't get to keep all the enjoyment for themselves. With support from the Canada Council, the Cultural Services Branch of the provincial government, and corporate sponsors, many of the major performing arts companies from Vancouver take their show on the road to urban centres around the province. Art exhibitions from major galleries and museums across Canada also tour small-town B.C. several times a year. In many communities, though, the real excitement is reserved for homegrown entertainment such as community theatre, which seems to grow stronger each year.

As the province's second major metropolis, Victoria has a vigorous and productive arts and entertainment community all its own with long-established institutions

cated in all regions of the province. These range from historical re-creations such as the fully restored gold rush village of Barkerville in the Cariboo or the 1890s fur trading post at Fort St. James on the Yellowhead Highway to major museums of international calibre such as the Royal B.C. Museum in Victoria and the UBC Museum of Anthropology. Known for the dramatic and involving quality of its exhibits, complete with sound effects, the Royal B.C. Museum attracts thousands of visitors a day and is the largest museum of its kind in Canada. The new UBC Museum of Anthropology is renowned both for the outstanding quality of its collection of Northwest Indian art and for the spectacular setting in which the collection is displayed.

But quality of life and culture aren't confined to museums, art galleries, or symphony orchestras. These facilities are important, but they would be dry and meaningless without the spirit of the people themselves. And the spirit of the people of B.C. shines through in thousands of ways each day—in the conversation in coffee shops and schoolyards in every corner of the province, in the tales people tell around the dinner table or the backyard barbeque, and in the way people help and encourage each other and try to improve their own lives and the lives of their family, friends, and neighbors.

ABOVE: Just one of British Columbia's many musical offerings, the Vancouver Symphony Orchestra plays to delighted audiences each season. Photo by Al Harvey/Masterfile

LEFT: Community theatre in British Columbia grows stronger every year as local residents discover the joys of the performing arts. Here, actors rehearse at the Capital Theatre in Nelson while the stage crew works on the production's scenery. Photo by Thomas Kitchin/First Light

FACING PAGE: Vancouver has developed into a world centre for the performing arts. From ballet and the symphony to theatre and the visual arts, British Columbia's arts community has something for everyone. Photo by Brian Milne/First Light

FOLLOWING PAGE: The UBC Museum of Anthropology is renowned for the outstanding quality of its collection of Northwest Indian art as well as for the spectacular setting in which the collection is displayed. Photo by Edward M. Gifford/Masterfile

# CHAPTER SIX

# A Look to the Future

by Jim Lyon

T oday British Columbia has a population of about 3 million, about half of whom live in the fast-growing Greater Vancouver region, where the hospitable climate, proximity to ocean and mountains, and breathtaking views conspire magnetically.

Whereas once Europe was predominant as a source of trade and immigrants, today the Pacific Rim nations capture the imagination of British Columbians. Trade between British Columbia and the Orient far exceeds business done with the countries of Europe, and newcomers from Asia have supplanted immigrants from the Old World. (While English and French are Canada's two official languages, it is not uncommon to see advertisements in English and Japanese in Vancouver hotels and stores.) The influx of well-educated, hard-working, and, often, affluent entrepreneurial Chinese from Hong Kong has made a particular impact on British Columbia. Fleeing Communist rule, which will begin in 1997, the Chinese from Hong Kong have brought their energy and capital to British Columbia, where they are developing a myriad of new businesses. They are the new shopkeepers, the professionals, and frequent winners of music festivals. While these new British Columbians are the most visible, others continue to be attracted to Canada's westernmost province from elsewhere in the

The grand Pan Pacific Hotel in Vancouver reaches toward the sky in a show of power and grace as British Columbia heads into its promising and vital future. Photo by Lorraine C. Parow/ First Light

BELOW: Futurists foresee no change in the status of Greater Vancouver as the engine of economic growth for the entire province of British Columbia. Visible in this skyline view of the city are False Creek and the Burrard Bridge. Photo by Brian S. Sytnyk/ Masterfile

RIGHT: More and more businesspeople and young professionals are choosing to leave the hectic pace of Toronto and Montreal for the more relaxed, yet vibrant atmosphere of Vancouver. Photo by Albert Chin/ First Light

FACING PAGE: Robson Square in Vancouver is a popular rendezvous spot for Vancouver's ever-growing population. Photo by Bill Brooks/ Masterfile

country. They are businessmen and young professionals weary of the hectic pace in Canada's biggest cities such as Toronto and Montreal, and farmers, who choose to escape the raw prairie winters by retiring to the benign climate of Vancouver Island to tend rose bushes in January. Three-quarters of the newcomers to British Columbia are Canadians, while 20 to 25 per cent are from other countries.

Life in British Columbia is good, and residents of the province know it, talk about it, and then show alarm when other people move to the region from overseas or from less congenial climates elsewhere in Canada.

Concern about the influx of newcomers is felt most keenly in Greater Vancouver, which has begun to exhibit classic symptoms of urban over-crowding. These problems are relative, however, since Vancouver's difficulties are far less acute than those faced by many cities with population densities far greater. Nevertheless, they are sufficiently pressing to command increasing public attention.

Greater Vancouver's difficulties are delineated by geography. The city and its adjoining municipalities are constrained from the west by the Strait of Georgia, from the north by mountains, and from the south by the U.S. border. Growth to the east into the wide, flat, and fertile Fraser Valley is restricted by a powerful piece of provincial legislation called the Agricultural Land Reserve. This legislation was designed to protect valuable farmland from urbanization.

In the past 25 years, the population in the Greater

Vancouver region has grown by two-thirds and is expected to increase from its present 1.4 million to 1.7 million by the year 2000. Although all parts of Greater Vancouver will experience population growth during the present decade, more than 60 per cent of the growth will likely occur in the suburbs in the eastern part of the region, particularly in the municipalities south of the Fraser River.

A study by the Greater Vancouver Regional District (GVRD) says if the high rate of migration experienced in recent years continues, the region's population may exceed 2 million by 2011. In addition, substantial growth is forecast for Fraser Valley communities such as Matsqui and Abbotsford, which are increasingly interconnected with the metropolitan area.

The GVRD study says this level of population growth may result in the need to find room for about 300,000 more households in Greater Vancouver. If current trends prevail, about two thirds could be single-family houses.

Unfortunately, Greater Vancouver has used much of its easily developable land in the past decades. As a result, the cost of both residential and industrial land can be expected to increase still further, and land less easily developed may have to be pressed into service at higher cost.

Inevitably, as readily developable land is used up, the pressure will intensify to use agricultural land for urban development.

New transportation links (high-speed ferries up the coast and across to Vancouver Island, expansions of the light-rapid transit rail system, and improved highways) will all help put Vancouver within commuting distance of areas which, today, are considered remote from British Columbia's biggest city.

LEFT: With a wealth of undeveloped land, British Columbia offers plenty of room for growth and development. This agricultural scene outside of Dawson Creek to the north reflects this abundance of land and space. Photo by J.A. Kraulis/Masterfile

ABOVE: The multibillion-dollar tourism industry of British Columbia adds to the continuing diversification of the provincial economy. This intrepid backpacker enjoys the trails of Nairn Falls Provincial Park. Photo by Gordon J. Fisher/ First Light

According to *The Vancouver Sun,* November 1990, the population of the Fraser Pacific region could increase by a million people (a population growth equivalent to two new Vancouvers) within the next 20 years. The Fraser Pacific region is a name the paper chose for an area that includes Whistler and the Sunshine Coast from Desolation Sound down through the Lower Mainland to Hope. There is certainly room for growth, but to be managed properly, it will require political will, much careful thought, and a more co-ordinated approach. The Pacific Fraser region, with an average density of 325 people per square kilometre, certainly is not overcrowded by worldwide standards. Tokyo, for example, has 9,100 people per square kilometre, London has 4,200, and Metropolitan Toronto has 3,400.

Futurists see Greater Vancouver remaining as the engine of economic growth for the province but, as transportation improves, industry will develop more in areas such as Kamloops and Kelowna in the interior, on Vancouver Island, and along the Sunshine Coast.

Demographers, who are concerned about long-term population changes, point to some interesting developments in British Columbia. More than 3 million people live in the province today. By the year 2011 there will likely be 4.1 million people living there.

Fertility rates in the province are falling short of the figure needed to sustain the population over the long term. It is thought that women of child-bearing age must have an average of 2.1 children to replace the existing population. In 1989, however, the fertility rate was only 1.7.

It is expected that British Columbia's population

will continue to experience a positive (although declining) natural increase until sometime around the year 2025. This is because a large proportion of the population is currently of child-bearing age. In 1990 it was expected that a natural increase would add about 18,500 infants to the province, or about 32 per cent of the total population increase for the year. By the year 2001 only 8,200 more people were expected to be born in the province than would die here, or about 16 per cent of the increase that was forecast.

British Columbia's population is aging. The median age of British Columbians in 1976 was just over 29 years. By the year 2011 this figure will have risen to over 40. Similarly, in 1976 there were 671 people of working age for every 100 people over the age of 65. By 2011 it is expected that every 100 retirees will be supported by only 413 people between the ages of 15 and 65.

Increased immigration could go some way toward mitigating (or at least delaying) the impact of an aging population. In 1988, for example, about 23 per cent of immigrants to Canada were under age 15.

An interesting study by the Economics Department of the B.C. Central Credit Union has pointed out that to cope with the aging population, the B.C. economy may have to make several adaptations.

Retirement may have to be delayed. With the median life expectancy in 2011 approaching 80 years (almost eight years longer than in 1976), the province may increasingly be unable to afford traditional retirement at age 65.

Education will become increasingly important as a smaller group of workers supports B.C.'s larger elderly population. To sustain living standards, the province must create jobs and industries that maximize the level of value added to their products. These industries need a sophisticated and well-educated work force.

Women and racial minorities will also become an increasingly vital component of the labor force, in both traditional and non-traditional occupations.

Richard Allen, the chief economist of B.C. Central Credit Union, wrote in 1990: "The changes to British Columbia's demographic profile are slow, and are relatively predictable. They are also, in large measure, intractable. These changes will require profound adjustments, and the time has come for the British Columbia economy to begin adapting to them."

Certainly much thought has been given to unshackling British Columbia from its traditional dependency on international commodity markets, where the

demand for products from the province's forests and mines is determined.

The spectacular growth of tourism, which, even today, only scratches the surface of a multibillion-dollar industry, and, to a lesser extent, the birth of an indigenous movie business, both point the way ahead to a more diversified economy.

Some of the province's best business, academic, and scientific minds have pondered the way ahead in a study, sponsored by the Science Council of British Columbia, of the economy up to the turn of the century. The study says that by the year 2000, the wealth generators in the provincial economy could be, in about equal parts: commodity resource products, value-added resource products, high-technology systems and products, international consulting, and tourism.

It is clear that while the forest sector will remain the driving force behind the economy, the nature of its resource is changing. Logging has been carried out in the mature forests of British Columbia for more than 125 years. Much of the old virgin forest is gone, and the

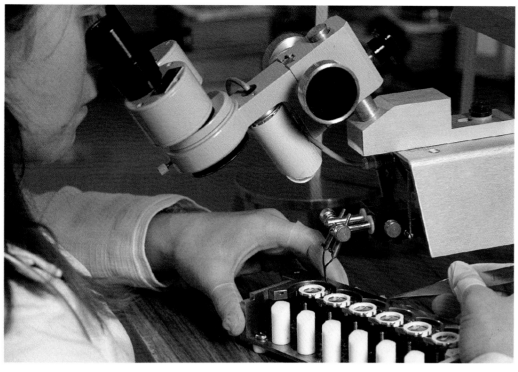

industry must adjust to handle the second growth of timber.

British Columbia has, as yet, little experience in handling second-growth forests. The Science Council says the opportunity exists to raise the potential growth of the province's forests by a full 50 per cent in a span of just 30 years. It even suggests that a doubling of the present growth may be biologically possible in 60 to 80 years.

Significant additional expenditures, however, will have to be made on research and development and for intensive forest management if these goals are to be achieved.

So far British Columbia has spent far less on forestry research and development than its competitors. This amounts to just over .26 per cent of sales. By comparison, the United States spends 1.5 per cent and Sweden spends 1.75 per cent.

It is argued that an investment of $100 million a year from governments and industry could increase the yield of wood dramatically (from 80 million to some 120 million cubic metres a year), sustain the present number of jobs in the forest industry (90,000 direct and 180,000 indirect), and enable the province to expand its exports.

ABOVE: In its study of the British Columbia economy, the Science Council has stated that within two to three decades an enormous biotechnology industry could flourish in the province. Photo by Albert Chin/First Light

LEFT: This pile of lodgepole pine and western white spruce will soon be entering a British Columbia sawmill for further processing. Lodgepole pine recently accounted for 25 percent of the provincial timber harvest. Photo by Thomas Kitchin/ First Light

FACING PAGE TOP: Since the forest industry is expected to maintain its status as the driving force behind the provincial economy well into the next century, British Columbia will be focusing on the research and development of second growth timber. A local nurseryman is shown here displaying the promising beginnings of a new western white spruce crop. Photo by Thomas Kitchin/First Light

Areas where increased research could be beneficial, according to the report, are in updating the forest inventory, learning more about the productivity of various sites, reforestation, development of new wood products, and ways to integrate forest management practices with other resource values and other uses of the land.

There was a time when little attention was paid to reforestation in British Columbia. Today, however, considerable emphasis is placed on the planting of new forests in areas denuded over past decades by wildfire, pests, disease, and harvesting and which were not satisfactorily restocked.

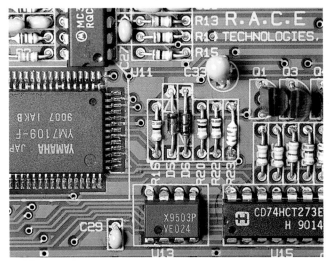

Soon nearly 300 million seedlings will be planted in a single year. In 1989 the second billionth seedling was planted. It took 50 years to plant the first billionth seedling and only seven years to plant the second. The third billionth seedling was expected to be planted in 1991.

Trees grow slowly in British Columbia. The first forests planted in the 1930s by British Columbians are only just ready for harvesting in the 1990s. Researchers, however, are working to shorten this growing cycle. They are developing genetically superior seedlings that are growing faster and will eventually produce higher-quality wood.

To develop genetically superior trees requires the gathering of high-quality seeds. Some species produce good cone crops only rarely. Spruce trees, for instance, produce cones in abundance only once in at least 12 years. When there is a good crop from species like spruce, forest workers make a special effort to gather lots of cones. A helicopter is often used. Dangling

beneath the hovering aircraft is a basket with a centre-opening rimmed with rake-like teeth. The basket is dropped over the tree's crown and, as the helicopter pulls up, the teeth strip off the cones and drop them into the basket.

Previously, in less sophisticated times, foresters obtained seed supplies from squirrel's caches or shot the cones from the treetops with a rifle equipped with telescopic sight.

The Science Council, in its study of the British Columbia economy, is enthusiastic about the potential for biotechnology. Once it begins to bear fully on the province's major resource and manufacturing industries, on its health care systems, and on its environment, a biotechnology industry will evolve within two to three decades whose economic value will exceed one billion dollars a year, says the Science Council.

Biotechnology has been around for many decades. It is used in wine making and beer brewing, in yogurt and cheese production, in the manufacture of antibiotics, vitamins, bakers yeast, and biological waste treatment. Ahead lies the manipulation of the genetic material in microbial, plant, animal, and human cells.

British Columbia's resource industries—forestry, mining, agriculture, fisheries, aquaculture, oil, and gas—are all potential candidates for the application of modern biotechnology. The growth of trees, agricultural crops, and livestock may be enhanced; losses may be reduced through the prevention of disease in tree seedlings, hatchery-reared salmon and trout, farm animals, and farm crops; and the protection of the environment against the impact of industrial activities.

One of the spectacular segments of the British Columbia economy has been information technology, which has grown in two decades to a one-billion-dollar industry with more than 750 companies employing about 11,500 people. Its growth is twice that of other manufacturing and primary resource-based industries, and it may well become British Columbia's third-largest industry (after forestry and tourism, but ahead of mining) before 1995.

A growing number of companies in the information technology industry in British Columbia are competing internationally in the areas of wireless and mobile communications, software applications, and in large systems integration contracts.

Dr. Denis Connor, former president of the Science Council, has said if information technology can sustain

the growth of 20 per cent a year, achieved for 12 years up to 1987-1988, it will become a sizable industry. "Twenty per cent a year on a $1 billion base is adding $200 million a year and 2,400 people in the first year, compounding thereafter. By the end of the decade you are talking $10 billion a year and 100,000 people, that's more people than the forest industry. And there is not any sign that this is not achievable. The biggest problem will be the lack of skilled people, who would be employed in these industries."

Clearly British Columbia faces an exciting future. The economy will be more diverse. There will be many more British Columbians, and they will come from different countries and different cultures. Transportation links will be expanded, and new population centres will develop. New special interest groups will emerge, representing the concerns of the province's growing ethnic communities. But British Columbia, facing westward toward the Pacific, will greet the new century with increasing confidence and assurance.

ABOVE: A diversified economy, room for continuing development, and a love for the land and its natural resources, will all help to see British Columbia achieve its full potential for prosperity and growth well into the future. Kitsilano Park in Vancouver is pictured here as the sun sets on another day in British Columbia. Photo by Al Harvey/Masterfile

FACING PAGE TOP: Fibre optics now play a major role in the communications industry in British Columbia. Photo by Norm Stelfox/First Light

FACING PAGE BOTTOM: Some of British Columbia's high-tech companies have developed the technology that has gone into the production of competitive circuit boards, which have helped to push Canada into the international computer industry market. Photo by Gordon J. Fisher/First Light

103

# PART TWO

# British Columbia's Enterprises

Evening descends over
the dynamic skyline of
Vancouver. Photo by
Thomas Kitchin/First
Light

# CHAPTER SEVEN

# Business and Professions

B ritish Columbia's professional community brings a wealth of service,
ability, and insight to the area.

Photo by Mark Tomalty

# The British Columbia Chamber of Commerce

The British Columbia Chamber of Commerce is an elected body of volunteers that provides a unified voice for all B.C. business, monitors government legislation, provides information and networking, and works for the economic diversification of the province.

The B.C. Chamber of Commerce, founded in 1951, is the only organization to represent all business in the province, and is the true "voice of business." It has spoken out on such vital issues as free trade, the goods and services tax, government spending and regulations, labor, and transportation.

For instance, the B.C. forest industry is increasingly controlled by huge multinational conglomerates. Current provincial government policies make it difficult for small, local entrepreneurs to compete. The chamber has recommended that the government study the forest industry, educate the public on the role of the natural resources in the provincial economy, and implement improvements to the present system.

Because of its heavy dependence on natural resources, B.C. is highly vulnerable to international events. The B.C. chamber has pressed provincial government to encourage development of secondary industries to stabilize the economy.

The B.C. chamber has spoken out on oil-spill prevention, liability insurance premiums, and

public procurement equality for small businesses. It prepared federal policy statements on reduction of the federal deficit, income tax simplification for small business, and fixed-rate, long-term financing.

Chamber members regularly receive updates on government proposals through chamber publications. They also receive summaries of chamber activities, executive summaries of all B.C. chamber submissions to government, and goverment response and position on chamber policy. Members can also request results of chamber research.

Information flows through the chamber from smaller members to the government. In the case of an extended B.C. rail strike, smaller communities in northern B.C.

**British Columbia is exceptional for its natural resources and its diversity.**

chamber organizes seminars and other forms of support, such as helping members actually deal with bureaucratic red tape by referring them directly to the correct official.

Generally, businesses are represented by the B.C. chamber through membership in their local chamber of commerce or board of trade. However, in areas where there is no local member body, companies can join the B.C. chamber directly.

Information on many provincial programs are distributed through the chamber network. Recently, a member found a market for its product in Seville, Spain. The firm learned from the chamber about a provincial program that provided the marketing assistance to establish business offshore.

were largely cut off from buyers and suppliers, creating hardships in remote areas. Through an efficient electronic networking system, the chamber made the federal government aware of these communities' difficulties.

Also, a small chamber can ask the provincial chamber for help with local problems with provincial/-federal implications. For instance, the B.C. chamber requested that the Ministry of Transportation and Highways quickly improve Highway 5 because of the fast economic growth of communities near the highway.

Establishing and organizing a local chamber can be difficult and time consuming. In recognition of the value of such groups to the well-being of the community and the province as a whole, the B.C.

Another provincial government program endorsed by the chamber is B.C. Marketplace, developed in response to business pressure to "help B.C. buyers find B.C. suppliers." The British Columbia Chamber of Commerce supports this initiative as one means of encouraging secondary industry and more stable economies in the province.

COIN (Canada Opportunities Investment Network) will have a similar effect. It is a nationwide database developed by provincial chambers of commerce across Canada to match up entrepreneurs with good ideas and investors with the capital to finance development of those ideas.

# Ebco Industries Ltd.

Hugo and Helmut Eppich, born in a German enclave in Yugoslavia, came to Canada in 1953. By 1956 they and a friend had saved $12,000—enough to start a tool and die makers shop in Vancouver. Helmut worked in the shop; Hugo helped during nights and weekends. Their first job, a bolt for B.C. Transformers sold for $4.35 (about half what it cost to make), but the firm was formed on a personal commitment to excellence. The first year's revenue was $10,000.

By 1966 Ebco (Eppich Brothers Company) had grown to 80 employees, consisting of 12 small companies and $2 million in sales growth; by 1976 there were 500 employees, 16 divisions, and $22 million sales growth. Today the private, Canadian-owned company, diversified and expanded, is, in the brothers' words, "a multicultural multiskilled mini-

The British Columbia "Entrepreneur of the Year" award was presented to Hugo and Helmut Eppich of the Ebco Group of Companies on April 24, 1990.

conglomerate," with annual revenues of approximately $100 million. The corporation now employs 900 people from nearly 50 different countries.

Ebco has earned a wide variety of awards, from product quality to human resource management presentations. Perhaps one of the most unusual was on June 9, 1989, when Hon. Gerry Weiner, Secretary of State of Canada, honored the company for its contributions to multiculturalism. Ebco takes a personal interest in the widely diversified customs and religions of their employees, an interest that has culminated in projects such as their annual Multicultural Food Festival, which symbolizes the ethnic diversity of Ebco's personnel, and the nine-metre high menorah that the Roman Catholic brothers donated to the Richmond synagogue.

In 1979 Ebco won a major contract with Boeing to build a 100-metre metal tube for its environmental laboratory. Unlike most companies, when Ebco realized a design change could produce the same quality tube at lower cost, they explained the idea to Boeing, saving the airplane manufacturer $368,000 off the contract price and becoming the first Canadian manufacturer to receive Boeing's cost-reduction award.

The company was the first non-American company to win Hughes Aircraft Superior Performance Award (1983), and the first company ever to win the award two years in a row (1984). Awards were presented to Ebco in 1984 by the federal and provincial governments for excellence for marketing for export (1984).

In 1990 B.C. Business Magazine selected the Eppich brothers as entrepreneurs of the year. The award credits much of the brothers' business success to their value system, which puts people first, followed closely by perfection, and in which prosperity takes care of itself.

In reality, all of the awards go back to the corporate value system. Diversity has been the hallmark of Ebco's growth and success; a focus on personal commitment to excellence has brought bigger and bigger customers to their doorstep, but "the value of the person," say the brothers, "is the very cornerstone of our corporate culture."

This value has extended all the way from employee awards to community involvement. Ebco has contributed to the arts, particularly metal sculptures. Ebco hosted an open house in 1975 to introduce their new Epic Data System, and to allow 2,500 visitors to view the 26-foot tunnel borer just completed for Yugoslavia. Ebco hosted a luncheon in October 1985 for Bill Bennett and 1,000 German-speaking British Columbians. Ebco employees donate money to the Richmond Food Bank—this company is a definite boon to the community.

Next in the value system, the value of perfection seems to include a "we can do it" attitude. This is exemplified by the brothers' commitment to provide satisfaction to the TRIUMF development.

Excited about the potential of TRIUMF, Ebco marketed aggressively to UBC in the early 1960s. In 1969 the firm signed its first major contract: construction of a stainless-steel vacuum tank and the aluminum resonators that constitute the heart of the TRIUMF cyclotron.

A tremendous challenge for a small company, the 60-foot diameter

LEFT: The centrepiece of the Ebco Aerospace facility in Delta, British Columbia, is the machining line. It consists of four SNK gantry profilers on the 13.3-by-190-foot bed.

BELOW: This giant plaque, located in the head office lobby, is a tribute to the many nationalities represented at Ebco Industries in Richmond, British Columbia.

techniques of accelerated training.

Individualized, competency-based learning materials seemed most promising. Ebco conducted several study trips to Canada, the United States, Britain, Germany, Switzerland, and Japan.

Internal training was to be individualized, competency-based, and organized into specialty modules of instruction, each focused on a specific skill area.

Unfortunately, the recession curtailed the program. However, many of the individualized, competency-based principles have been adopted by the independent non-profit ITEK (formerly EPIC) industrial training centre that serves the specialized training needs of the entire manufacturing sector in the Lower Mainland. Once again, Ebco has pioneered research and development that provides lasting benefits to the industrial community as a whole.

In another sideline from the TRIUMF success, Ebco signed a technology transfer agreement with the research facility in 1987, allowing them to use their newly learned cyclotron technology to develop a smaller, moderately priced cyclotron that could be sold to hospitals and medical centres for on-site production of the rapidly disintegrating isotopes so vital to medical research and analysis. Within only two years, Ebco had a promising first product on the market.

tank had to be capable of withstanding high temperatures and maintaining an atom-free internal vacuum. The trick was to seal the interior so no molecules of gas could slip in from the encircling metals, including the welds. To accommodate this project, Ebco expanded its facilities, brought in experts to retrain 16 stainless-steel welders and 16 aluminum welders, adapted new quality-control assurance methods, and devised innovative new electroplating technologies. Ebco's first tank withstood the test.

Not only had they won the TRIUMF contract and succeeded, they had acquired the technologies for two new branches of business. The data collection and analysis technologies developed for their quality-control program inspired industrial products for a new satellite firm, Epic Data, Inc., established in 1974 and open to the public in 1975, selling to major corporations such as the Montreal Post Office by 1978.

In the late 1970s Ebco was faced with acute skills shortages. They used the local apprenticeship system to train new tradesmen, but this training could not meet immediate corporate needs. So the firm began extensive research into the latest

The future looks good for the new Ebco Industries. Their cyclotron may become one component of "packaged" imaging centres to be sold to hospitals and health centres around the world.

And it looks equally good for this vibrant mini-conglomerate with the high corporate values that have created employee loyalty, product excellence, and a team spirit that produces "yes we can" results.

# Dairyland Foods

In 1990 the Fraser Valley Milk Producers Cooperative Association (FVMPCA), popularly known as Dairyland Foods, was selected as one of British Columbia's top 20 private companies, proving that co-operatives can work. With 1,500 employees and more than $450 million estimated revenues in that year, Dairyland is the largest home-owned food products manufacturer in B.C. Nonetheless, it is a relatively small company when competing with immense multinational corporations. Its survival depends on innovative ser-

**RIGHT:** Dairyland Foods is well known for its wide range of products. From dairy items to juices, this company's products are synonymous with excellence.

**BELOW:** Milk is shipped directly from the members of Fraser Valley Milk Producers Cooperative Association to processing facilities, guaranteeing freshness and quality. The association, celebrating its 75th year in business in 1991, uses the corporate name Dairyland Foods to market products.

vice to customers and business profits for its farmer-members.

The FVMPCA originated as a producer-driven initiative in the early 1900s. Historically, Fraser Valley dairy farmers had hauled milk to Vancouver distributors in horse-drawn carts. When the B.C. Electric Railway completed its line to Chilliwack in 1910 and Canadian National completed a Vancouver link soon after, there was a faster, more economical way to bring Fraser Valley milk to the coast. However, excess supplies made it possible for dealers to slash prices by playing one farmer against another. Despite their fierce independence, Fraser Valley dairymen soon realized they would have to unite to

RIGHT: The extensive distribution network that Dairyland Foods has developed meets the needs of customers throughout the province.

BELOW: Dairyland Foods' modern production facilities and plant sanitation programs ensure that all products meet the highest standard of quality.

survive, and the Fraser Valley Milk Producers Cooperative Association was formed in 1913.

The initiative was slowed by World War I, but the more aggressive members continued canvassing and raising funds. In 1919 the association bought its first two processing facilities, the Chilliwack and Edenbank Creameries, and a retail organization, Standard Dairy Company of Vancouver.

The association has always sought to maintain leadership in developing quality products. In 1923 it became the first in Canada to employ a dairy bacteriologist; in 1925 it became first to establish a commercial dairy laboratory to ensure milk quality.

The Dairyland brand was introduced in 1943. In 1964 Dairyland completed its $3.75-million head office and plant in Burnaby, and in 1968 it purchased its first plant outside the Lower Mainland/Fraser Valley region, the Kitimat Dairy. Today it owns nine plants and 27 distribution centres throughout the province, serving nearly every small community in B.C., from southwestern B.C. and the Kootenays to Prince Rupert and the Yukon, and 70 percent of B.C.'s dairy farmers are FVMPCA member-owners.

As well as providing product quality and customer service, a successful co-operative must make a concerted effort to create a viable business climate for its members—in this case,

the dairy farmers. Business security for B.C. dairymen is still a prime company objective. The organization works with and for farmers on government relations, industry regulation, free trade, taxes, and many such matters that the individual farmers lack the expertise or the time to manage.

On a local level, dairy farmers in many regions of B.C. have benefited from joining the co-operative. In the Bulkley Valley, joining FVMPCA gave producers access to a modern processing plant at Smithers, which in turn helped keep the dairy industry alive in that region. In the early 1980s Dairyland merged with NOCA, the debt-ridden North Okanagan Cooperative Association, and has since managed to rejuvenate the business there.

On the client-oriented side of its success, product quality and customer satisfaction are vital to Dairyland Foods. But to succeed in today's competitive markets, a successful company must go well beyond those parameters. It is Dairyland's goal not only to meet, but to

exceed customer expectations.

For instance, Dairyland provides a service that is rare today—home delivery—with a twenty-first century twist. Not only do the drivers deliver more than 300 milk and other grocery products, but they also collect any of their used plastic containers for recycling. Manager Tom Low declares customer response to have been outstanding, and Dairyland is moving toward several other environmental initiatives for the 1990s.

Low explains, "We make every effort to be responsive to growing needs. Our future will depend entirely on how well we meet our customer requirements."

# Andersen Consulting

We live in the information age. Our success depends on how well we use increasingly valuable information resources. It is more and more crucial to master and utilize information technology to link people and technologies to solve the problems of increased global competition.

Andersen Consulting in Vancouver has strong ties to the international sector, particularly Seattle and Portland. Such ties enable Andersen Consulting to form long-term business partnerships with large and complex corporations such as B.C. Tel, B.C. Gas, B.C. Hydro, and various government ministries.

Bill Evenden, partner in charge of the Vancouver office, explains, "Our unified, multinational practice enables us to think global but act local. We bring the collective knowledge, expertise, and resources of the worldwide organization to each local client engagement."

Andersen Consulting is unique in its global reach. The largest management information consulting company in the world, it draws on a

**Andersen Consulting professionals receive more than 1,000 hours of rigorous training in their first five years.**

wide base of international resources when helping corporations develop the integrated solutions necessary to remain competitive in today's complex business environment.

As part of the Arthur Andersen Worldwide Organization, Andersen Consulting has over 20,000 employees and 794 partners in 150 offices in 49 countries. Its mission is to empower organizations (and individuals) to use technology to their business advantage. Its consulting services range from computer-software design and installation and systems integration and management to strategic information planning, systems productivity consulting, strategic consulting, and change management services.

Andersen maintains its competitive advantage with professional training, a commitment to research and development (R&D), and community involvement.

Each year the firm spends $137 million in personnel development. In their first five years with the firm, each consultant receives over 1,000 hours of training in systems development methodology, advanced business techniques, and state-of-the-art technology. Ongoing professional development keeps them on the leading edge of the information age.

Andersen Consulting invests more than $250 million each year in R&D. The firm's proprietary software packages and services grew out of its R&D efforts.

The company encourages its employees to be active members of the community. In 1989 the company donated services to design and install new hardware and software systems for recording and processing all the in-

**Andersen Consulting installed the first commercial computer system in America in 1954. Since then Andersen Consulting has grown into the world's largest systems-consulting organization.**

formation needed to run the United Way campaign accurately and speedily. Rose O'Connel of United Way says, "Andersen's people were terrific. We couldn't have done it without them."

Long a United Way supporter, Andersen Consulting in Vancouver has received the campaign's Employee Gold Award every year since 1983. Andersen has also sponsored events by the Vancouver Symphony Orchestra and Vancouver Opera, and it contributes to the Management Information Systems Excellence Fund at the University of British Columbia.

# B.C. Pavilion Corporation

B.C. Pavilion Corporation manages some of the world's best convention and meeting facilities. Through careful research, innovative ideas, carefully targeted marketing, and "yes we can" service, the corporation is successfully selling its facilities in competitive world markets.

The corporation, directly responsible to the provincial Ministry of Development, Trade and Tourism, manages B.C. Place Stadium, Robson Square Conference Centre, the Bridge Studios, the B.C. Transportation Museum, the Vancouver Trade & Convention Centre, and TRADEX (Fraser Valley Trade and Exhibition Centre) at the Abbotsford Airport—opening July 1991.

The beautiful Trade & Convention Centre on the city's shoreline offers first-class banquet facilities for up to 7,000 guests and 94,000 square feet of column-free exhibition space, an adjoining 17,000-square-foot ballroom, and 21 meeting rooms. In world markets many centres offer these amenities. However, not many places can offer a clean, safe city along with the splendor of Vancouver's north-shore mountains, the proximity to recreation areas such as Whistler, the colorful cultural mosaic of B.C.'s population, and an excellent international location, all in one package. Through marketing these amenities, B.C. Pavilion Corporation has filled the Vancouver Trade & Convention Centre to 53 percent of capacity within three years, when the national convention capacity average is only 47 percent.

Smart marketing brings the clients a commitment to service beyond their expectations and keeps them coming back. For instance when the opera spectacular, AIDA, was coming to Vancouver, B.C. Place Stadium facilities were more than adequate for the event's huge sets and live elephants. However, Vancouver's streets were too narrow to allow access, so staff arranged for barge transportation up False Creek inlet. Such commitment to service helped to make B.C. Place Stadium the best-attended, highest-revenue entertain-

The Vancouver Trade & Convention Centre, with its unique five-sail roof, has been making waves in the convention business since it opened in July 1987.

ment facility in Canada in 1989 and the sixth highest in North America.

In only three years this organization has brought to Vancouver such world-renowned events as varied as the Inter Comm Telecommunication Congress & Exhibition, the Molson Indy auto race, the Children's Winter Festival (WinterFest), and a wide variety of other international conventions.

Since the convention market appears to be softening, B.C. Pavilion Corporation is shifting emphasis to trade and consumer shows, combined convention/trade shows, special events, sports, and entertainment. Already it has lined up more than $110 million in confirmed future bookings for the Vancouver Trade & Convention Centre, many of them international events that will bring global marketing opportunities to the doorstep of Vancouver businesses.

The 60,000-seat B.C. Place Stadium is the largest domed stadium in the world. The stadium, which opened in June 1983, is the perfect setting for trade and consumer shows, concerts, and sporting events.

# Williams Moving & Storage

George James Williams borrowed $50 from his landlord in 1929 to purchase a Dodge touring van and start business. By 1990 the company, headed by son George, had 21 offices in Western Canada, was a member of United Van Lines, and had affiliations with moving companies around the world.

When it was incorporated as Williams Moving and Storage Ltd. in 1949, the company operated seven trucks and one trailer for cross-Canada hauls. In the early 1950s Williams began building a network of branches across British Columbia and into Alberta and expanded national hauling through affiliation with United Van Lines (Canada) Ltd.

Acquisition of Robertson Moving and Storage Limited, with offices in Calgary, Edmonton, and Grande Centre, made Williams the largest privately owned moving company in Western Canada by 1971 and big enough to sign a contract with Sears Canada, Inc., in 1973. Starting with four tractor units and 12 trailers for deliveries throughout British Columbia, this contract now covers B.C., the Yukon, Alberta, Saskatchewan, Manitoba, and northeast to Thunder

Bay, Ontario, using 85 tractors and 290 trailers.

Always at the forefront, Williams Moving pioneered use of containers for moving and storage, and at the suggestion of employee Glenn Thompson of Terrace, it developed double container trailers for use in Western Canada. Williams also contributed time and trucking expertise to Project Miles, a two-year test of the clean-burning methanol fuel developed by Sypher Mueller

George "Sonny" Williams succeeded his father as president of Williams Moving & Storage in 1971.

International, Inc.

Williams was a sponsor for the B.C. Open Golf Tournament for eight years, at the same time raising money for B.C.'s disabled children. In 1989 it became both a corporate sponsor and an official carrier for the B.C. Summer Games.

Today Williams Moving & Storage is the number-one mover in B.C., Alberta, and Saskatchewan and is top mover for the federal government. Affiliated with United Van Lines, it is number one across Canada and has now expanded into international markets. The newest company branch, Williams Moving International, markets to corporations, moving personnel and goods across the continent and around the world.

LEFT: This combination—a van towing a 27-foot "pup" trailer with containers— is typical of the efficient equipment used by Williams Moving & Storage today.

BELOW: Williams Moving & Storage containers are vital to the large, growing business of moving people internationally. Special equipment is used to handle the containers at the docks.

# Seaboard Life Insurance Company

Seaboard Life Insurance Company is a Canadian-based company, the largest life insurance group with a head office in Vancouver. Seaboard's financial performance has grown strongly over the past five years, showing nearly 175 percent growth in revenues. In a single year, 1990, company assets increased by more than 25 percent to $973 million. Net income for that year exceeded $4.2 million.

The parent company, Friends' Provident Life Office of London, England, has a strong financial history. Founded in 1832, Friends'

These are some of the different policies that have been issued over the years. On the right is a "Jubilee" policy issued by Saskatchewan Life in 1935, and to the left is the original nonsmokers' policy issued by Seaboard Life in 1980.

Provident currently has assets of $15 billion and business contacts around the world, providing an excellent support system for the Vancouver company.

Seaboard's chief executive officer, J. Stewart Cunningham, joined Friends' Provident in the early 1950s, and came to Canada when that company bought majority control of Fidelity Life of Regina in 1957. Cunningham moved to the West Coast with Fidelity two years later, when its head office was moved to

Vancouver to take advantage of the city's proximity to American and Pacific Rim markets and its rapidly growing economy.

In 1983 Friends' Provident bought majority control of Seaboard Life Insurance Company. In 1986 Fidelity Life and Seaboard Life amalgamated under the Seaboard name. Friends' Provident had acquired Fidelity Life in 1957. The original name of this company had been Saskatchewan Life and the name was changed in 1942. Saskatchewan Life originally opened for business in Regina, Saskatchewan, in 1914.

Seaboard Life operates three marketing divisions. The individual marketing division distributes individual insurance and annuity policies in Canada and the western United States. Its distributors are independent agents and the company is well known for innovative products. For instance it was the first company in Canada to introduce a nonsmoker's policy. This division is organized to allow the maximum autonomy in the regional offices to service the local agents, and a telephone hot-line and state-of-the-art computer system allow distributors quick contact with the head office, providing instant customized financial plans for clients.

Seaboard Life's SAL programme, long a leader and innovator in after-sales service for the Canadian automotive industry, has also consistently moved strongly ahead. The company introduced a new version of SAL 4000 in 1989, a comprehensive after-sales and marketing support package that provides the innovative PROFIT (Performance Review of Finance Today) programme that includes training to increase management skills of dealerships' business managers and sales staff and a test to assist in hiring managers and staff.

Seaboard Life Insurance Company is the largest life insurance group with a head office in Vancouver.

The company's special marketing division has been a major underwriter of student accident policies for school boards across Canada, and the company is fast becoming a prominent underwriter of special risk insurance for staff of colleges and universities. Special risk insurance also offers coverage in areas as diverse as underwater exploration of the Atlantic coast or helicopter logging along the Pacific coast.

Seaboard opened an office in the United States in 1981. In 1986 the company moved more aggressively into the huge American market, and it is now licensed in 12 states, with offices in Washington, Oregon, and California.

The company credits much of its success to its employees. They help to fulfil the corporate slogan STRIVE (Service, Teamwork, Responsibility, Integrity, Value, and Excellence). It is the employees' dedication to customer service and innovation that provides the company with its competitive advantage.

# CHAPTER EIGHT

# Quality of Life

Educational, service, and communication institutions contribute to the
quality of life of British Columbia
residents and visitors alike.

Photo by Pat Morrow

# B.C. Ministry of Environment

British Columbia's economy is based on its abundant natural resources. This fact, matched with growing public concern over what happens to the environment when resources are exploited, has made the province a leader in the development of ecologically sound economic development.

The Ministry of Environment is a key agency in this effort. Environment Minister Dave Mercier says, "The provincial government is serious about protecting, restoring, and enhancing the integrity, diversity, and quality of British Columbia's natural ecosystems and human environments."

"This includes maximizing the social and economic benefits available through the province's resources," adds Mercier.

Ministry priorities include cleanup of existing damage to the environment, prevention of future problems through reduction and control of waste and other threats to ecosystems, and conservation of resources.

One of the higher-profile ministry initiatives is its participation in an international oil-spill task force. British Columbia took the lead in forming this organization, which now includes the governments of Alaska, Washington State, Oregon, and California.

In addition, the ministry has developed a Provincial Oil Spill Response Strategy which outlines British Columbia's roles and responsibilities in the event of a marine oil spill and provides funding for related equipment and training programs.

The ministry is working with Washington State to develop joint programs on a variety of other common environmental concerns.

This kind of innovative thinking is also reflected in research currently under way at the University of British Columbia. The program, using $900,000 from provincial lottery funds, is exploring ways of avoiding pollution from acid mine drainage and forest industry wastewater.

To ensure that new industrial operations are as environmentally "friendly" as possible, the Ministry of Environment participates in the Major Project Review Process (MPRP), which it administers in cooperation with the Ministry of Development, Trade, and Tourism. The MPRP revolves around a committee assigned to review plans for pulp and paper mills, mineral smelting and refining plants, chemical operations, and major port and marine developments. The committee, made up of representatives from the ministries of Forest; Energy, Mines, and Petroleum Resources; and Municipal Affairs, Recreation, and Culture, as well as the two "parent" ministries, looks at the ecological and social impacts of every proposal before permits or licenses are issued. This results in clear guidance for industry

The Environment Youth Corps program puts young people to work on a variety of projects to help keep British Columbia green.

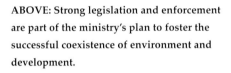

ABOVE: Strong legislation and enforcement are part of the ministry's plan to foster the successful coexistence of environment and development.

RIGHT: The Ministry of Environment is serious about protecting, restoring, and enhancing British Columbia's ecosystems.

on regulatory requirements through a single government source.

British Columbia now has some of the toughest anti-pollution laws in the country. Those found to be intentionally damaging the environment are subject to a maximum fine of $3 million and a three-year jail term. In 1991 provincial conservation officers investigated nearly 8,000 suspected offenders and laid more than 4,000 charges against operations and individuals found to be acting against environmental legislation.

Strong legislation and enforcement are only part of the government plan to foster the successful coexistence of environment and development. The Ministry of Environment is also implementing several initiatives to en-

courage industry, government bodies, and private citizens to reduce, re-use, and recycle waste materials.

Among these initiatives is the Environmental Industries Strategy, established to encourage new industries in British Columbia to serve as markets for recycled wastes. The plan identifies existing and potential environmental industries, products, and opportunities. This information has been entered into an extensive database which may be accessed through a province-wide, toll-free waste exchange hotline. A computerized Environmental Enterprise Database has also been set up on the international British Columbia Business Network.

Public awareness is essential to the success of any environmental improvement program. One major step to that end is a travelling educational exhibit which uses interactive computer games, color graphics, and a video presentation, to involve school-children and their parents in helping to keep British Columbia beautiful.

Another unique initiative activated by the ministry is the Envi-

ronment Youth Corps. Established by the provincial government in May 1989, the Youth Corps program puts young people to work on a wide variety of "green" projects. To date, Youth Corps crews have built waste disposal boxes, restored a rocky beach environment for blennies (an eel-like fish), conducted fish surveys and assisted with oil-spill response, among other activities.

Along with the satisfaction gained from helping improve British Columbia's environment, those participating in the Environment Youth Corps program receive on-the-job training in areas such as first aid, wildlife enhancement, forestry, tourism, and construction.

The British Columbia Ministry of Environment is working hard to preserve the beauty of this province for the benefit and pleasure of future generations. Stewardship of this "living legacy" is something every member of the British Columbia Environment team takes very seriously.

# Women's Programs

In acknowledgment of the barriers of advancement faced by women throughout British Columbia, the provincial government has established the Ministry of Women's Programs and Government Services and Minister Responsible for Families. This ministry promotes equal opportunities for all women within the province.

Early in 1990 Carol Gran, Minister of Women's Programs, conducted a province-wide tour and mail-out survey which reached more than 60,000 women. She then appointed an Advisory Council on Community-Based Programs for Women to consider the priority issues for British Columbia women and to recommend strategies for improvements. Together, these forums provided the minister with a clear picture of the needs of women from all backgrounds and at all levels of British Columbia society.

Using this information as a basis, Women's Programs will continue to promote programs and policies that build equal economic, social, and political opportunities for women both within government and the private sector. It provides support to all government ministries, distributes information on women's issues, and sponsors a Women's Grants Program, which funds non-profit community organizations also working to enhance opportunities for women.

One of the first major achievements since the minister's consultation process is the implementation of pay equity in the provincial public service. Male- and female- dominated job groups are currently being assessed in terms of skill, effort, responsibility, and working conditions. After these two groups are com-

Women's Programs staff and clients meet at the ministry information booth.

The Honourable Carol Gran, minister responsible for government management services and minister responsible for Women's Programs, province of British Columbia.

pared, pay equity will be achieved through wage adjustments negotiated between the government and the public sector unions.

As many as 13,000 employees will benefit from pay equity, 80 percent of them women. The program is expected to cost $40 million, and will be phased in over four years, beginning in January 1991.

One of the stumbling blocks to advancement for many women is a lack of affordable, quality child care. Without adequate child care, many women in B.C. with small children are unable to access employment

opportunites or education and training programs. Minister of Women's Programs, Carol Gran, has established a Child Care Team to address this issue. The purpose of the team is to oversee and speed up the expansion of child care programs throughout the province.

Another major focus of Women's Programs is the issue of family violence in British Columbia. The Provincial Task Force on Family Violence, established by Gran, is investigating ways to reduce violence against women, children, and the elderly and to improve government policies, programs, and services for victims of family violence. The ministry also works directly with communities to help them assess their local needs and improve their services for women.

Women's Programs recognizes the need to assess the impact of current and future government policies on women, and to develop the means to ensure equal representation of women in all decision-making bodies.

# B.C. Round Table on Environment and Economy

The Round Table is made up of British Columbians from all walks of life, united to resolve the province's environmental, social, and economic concerns.

British Columbia has responded to the challenge of sustainable economic development by establishing a permanent Round Table on Environment and Economy. Reporting to the Cabinet Committee on Sustainable Development co-chaired by the minister of environment and the minister of Development, Trade, and Tourism, the Round Table has excited international interest.

A multidisciplinary advisory body to the provincial cabinet, its main function is to make recommendations on a sustainable development strategy. In addition to the sustainable development strategy, the Round Table will also be expected to recommend techniques for dispute resolution, and to heighten public understanding and knowl-edge of sustainable development.

British Columbia, with its resource-based economy, has been concerned for decades about long-term implications of harvesting those resources. In 1987, shortly after the World Commission on Environment and Development, chaired by the Norwegian prime minister, Madame Gro Harlem Brundtlandy, released its world report, British Columbia had its own task force in place, headed by Dr. David Strangway of UBC. The Strangway report, released in the summer of 1989, recommended a permanent Round Table on Environment and Economy, and the B.C. government announced establishment of the Round Table the following January.

Currently, the group is gathering information and ideas from industry, interest groups, and concerned agencies throughout the province, as part of the process of developing a sustainable development strategy. Once the strategy is in place, the Round Table will remain as an independent body, to provide advice to Cabinet on matters related to the environment, land use, and economic development.

Sustainable development is a complex issue, requiring a fine balance between economic needs and the need to preserve natural resources. Public awareness is a vital factor in the success of this initiative, and will be a long-term process, involving many government and nongovernment agencies.

Members of the Round Table are well qualified for their task. The 31 appointees come from a wide range of interest groups and industries, including environmental groups, forestry, fishing, mining, tourism, labor unions, local governments, native people, and academia. They were appointed from a list of nominees put forth by various agencies and interest groups, and will hold office for three-year terms.

# British Columbia Telephone Company (B.C. Tel)

"We're connected. We have communication across the nation at the speed of light"—B.C. Tel chairman Gordon MacFarlane, March 13, 1990.

With these words, MacFarlane announced completion of the British Columbia portion of the Trans-Canada Lightguide Transmission System, a technology so advanced that it could become a viable, environmentally sound alternative to the physical movement of people.

The Lightguide Transmission System is unaffected by temperature changes or electromagnetic fields, and will be far more efficient than regular telephone transmission systems in current use. This new system can transmit the information contained in 32 volumes of the Encyclopedia Britannica, including pictures, in less than a second. It will support fully in-

**One hair-thin pair of fibre-optic strands can transmit the information contained in 32 volumes of the Encyclopedia Britannica, including pictures, in less than one second.**

teractive, full-motion video conferencing with as much privacy and security as if the participants were in the same room. Over fibre-optic lines, a Vancouver executive can electronically hand his Toronto counterpart the set of figures and graphs they are discussing, or he can attend a seminar in Halifax from his own office.

B.C. Tel has come a long way since it began as a small telephone company in 1891. In 1913 the firm received authorization to expand to all parts of British Columbia, and in 1923 it was incorporated nationally under federal charter as B.C. Telephone Company Limited. The business has continued to grow with the population of the province, a growth that is still occurring. At 72 percent digital and 76 percent electronic, B.C. Tel's network today is one of the most advanced in North America. It brings telephone service to 99 percent of the province's populated areas, including mobile facilities that provide the most remote regions with high-quality communication.

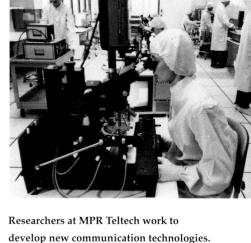

**Researchers at MPR Teltech work to develop new communication technologies.**

No longer only a telephone service, B.C. Tel has become Canada's second-largest telecommunications company, and has connecting agreements that make it one of the few world-scale competitors in the telecommunications industry.

The key to success has been ongoing customer service. During the past two decades customer needs and expectations have changed dramatically. In order to respond adequately to this market pull, B.C. Tel has made major corporate changes.

Remaining on the leading edge of technology has been the big challenge. B.C. Tel established the subsidiary MPR Teltech to develop new communications technologies and innovative applications for business and government. Among other things, this division is working on the satellite communications system that has put B.C. Tel at the forefront of portable communications, and that continues to be a base for future developments.

Other leading-edge technologies include developments in broadband and fibre optics, which support international data systems, on-line services, and electronic networking. Innovative network architectures

provide rapid, flexible, secure communication systems for front-line corporations.

As B.C. Tel develops new technologies, it rapidly diversifies into new markets. Globalization of industry, rapidly changing business needs, and tremendous expansion in the information industry are creating both challenges and opportunities for the company. There has been a marked increase in the demand for facsimile systems and credit verification systems. Satellite communications have made high-quality portable communications systems an expected part of everyday life. Globally active corporations require fast, reliable data transmission services; demand is growing for worldwide video conferencing as a vital management tool.

During the 1980s, B.C. Tel concentrated on strengthening its abilities to respond to changing demands of business clients, both in developing research and development capabilities and in working with its employees. Basically a service industry, the firm recognizes that its most valuable resource is a loyal, capable work force. Company growth has included development of structures to meet changing employee requirements, and acceleration of ongoing employee training and equipment upgrading to help its people obtain greater job satisfaction and provide even better customer service.

B.C. Tel is entering the 1990s with fully established research and development facilities, an integrated systems and consulting division, and a solid footing in cellular technology.

The firm is well positioned in terms of people, technology, and strategies to play a major role in further development of the information industry in the coming decade. Its technological push in broadband and other areas such as wireless

ABOVE: B.C. Tel's province-wide network is one of the most advanced in North America.

RIGHT: Satellite communications mean that even remote communities have access to high-quality telecommunications.

communication and software-defined network architecture positions it to respond to the market pull for sophisticated information transmission. Chief executive officer Brian Canfield predicts a bright future for the company: "We expect the demand for communications services to continue to grow as the information sector of the economy continues to expand. As international competitiveness modifies business practices, as energy costs rise, as environmental awareness grows, our telecommunications substitutes for the physical movement of information and people will become progressively more economic."

B.C. Tel built 800 kilometers of the Trans-Canada Lightguide Transmission System at a cost of some

$116 million. The line runs through some of the most rugged terrain in the world, crossing three mountain ranges, travelling through coastal rainforest and high desert plains and across hundreds of rivers and streams, and was finished eight months ahead of schedule.

Throughout the project, B.C. Tel took care to safeguard the wild beauty of its home province. In 1989 it received commendation for these efforts in the form of environmental awards from both the B.C. Ministry of Environment and the Association of Professional Engineers of B.C.

# Wedgewood

From the uniformed valet at the front door to the understated elegance of the decor, Vancouver's Wedgewood Hotel exudes the quality of a luxury European hotel. Personalized service gives the hotel a competitive edge, and its location near the heart of Vancouver's business, entertainment, and shopping centre attracts business and leisure clientele alike, though the hotel caters primarily to business travellers.

The hotel's success can be attributed largely to highly personalized service, and the hands-on management style of owner-manager Eleni Skalbania, who has worked 12- to 16-hour days since the

**Wedgewood's success can be attributed in part to the efforts of owner-manager Eleni Skalbania.**

Wedgewood's beginnings.

Skalbania managed the Devonshire Hotel and then the Georgia for a short time during the 1970s and early 1980s. At that time she perceived that, despite the abundance of hotels in Vancouver, the city lacked a good-quality, European-style luxury hotel. An extensive traveller herself, she noted the best features of hotels around the world, and from them created her own concept of personalized hospitality.

In 1983 Skalbania had an opportunity to realize her dream when she obtained a lease on the Mayfair Hotel. The Mayfair was badly run down, but the location was good, right in the heart of Vancouver. She allowed six months and $4 million for renovations, designing and redesigning every detail herself. The entire building was gutted-out and rebuilt, and Skalbania supervised it all. Antiques and art pieces from her own private collection provided finishing touches, and in June 1984, on schedule and under budget, the Wedgewood opened its doors.

"I was lucky, because it was a good time to be doing renovations," says Skalbania. "In 1983 the economy was in a recession and the hotels were not doing well. I was able to get good contracts."

To be profitable, a small hotel must have high year-round occupancy rates, and the only place to obtain that is in the corporate market. With this in mind, the entire Wedgewood

advertising budget was directed toward the corporate market in British Columbia, Alberta, and Ontario.

A few other factors helped. When the hotel was ready to start business, the Vancouver economy was turning upward after a slump. Many of Skalbania's clientele from the two previous hotels followed her to the Wedgewood. The novelty of a European-style hotel in Vancouver caught the imagination of the media, and they provided excellent coverage of this new-to-Vancouver concept. British Columbia's burgeoning movie industry loved this small, exquisite hotel with its personalized service. Business from that source included big-name stars such as Tom Selleck, Sean Connery, Gina Lollobrigida, Kirstie Alley, and Burt Reynolds, bringing the hotel an additional high-profile image.

Within three months the Wedgewood had reached 90-percent occupancy and had surpassed projected revenues. Within two years Skalbania was able to purchase the property outright.

The Wedgewood still caters primarily to the corporate market. One step at a time, sales and marketing director Joanna Tsaparas has extended the reach, first across Canada, then into the United States and Europe. The hotel now draws clients from New Zealand and Australia as well, and plans are being made to move into other Pacific Rim countries as they open up.

Much of the hotel's success comes from repeat business. "Personal service is the key to our success," explains Skalbania.

The Wedgewood provides personalized service, from the 24-hour room service to the valet parking and maid service twice daily. For those who want it, breakfast is brought to the door of their room, complete with the morning paper.

To facilitate superb personalized service, the hotel employs 120 trained people, slightly above the average one-to-a-room rate for luxury hotels. Wedgewood staff members recognize frequent guests, and computerized guest profiles ensure consistent satisfaction for repeat clients. Above all, Skalbania personally acknowledges her guests' loyalty and their needs.

The hotel offers both individual and corporate services. Three airy banquet rooms, each opening onto an attractive garden terrace, are available for corporate functions, and business travellers can access complete secretarial services in the hotel. An adjacent health club provides squash courts, weight room, and sauna/whirlpool facilities for relaxation.

Each of the 94 rooms has its own flower-bedded balcony, some have fireplaces, two or three phones, make-up mirrors, hair dryers, and plush bathrobes. A mini-bar and in-

ABOVE: Vancouver's Wedgewood Hotel exudes the quality and luxury of a European-style hotel.

LEFT: Each of the hotel's 94 rooms has its own flower-bedded balcony and is appointed with the most luxuriant furnishings.

dividually controlled heating and air conditioning add to the luxurious treatment.

The Bacchus restaurant has become a favorite meeting place for the Vancouver lunchtime crowd and a popular dining spot in the evening. Its excellent Northern Italian food in an atmosphere of country-style elegance, dancing, and live entertainment make every visit a special one.

# Ministry of Advanced Education, Training, and Technology-International Education

More and more overseas corporations, educational institutions, national governments, and individuals are becoming aware of the value and variety of educational experiences available in British Columbia. Whether it is training in the trades, a diploma in business administration, high-tech expertise, or English language training, the necessary educational services are available at one or more of the public post-secondary education institutions in this province.

Most of British Columbia's three universities, 16 colleges, four provincial institutes, and the Open Learning Agency are exporting their expertise throughout the world. Together they participate in more than $64-million worth of international education projects. In Indonesia alone, consultants from British Columbia have participated in a $7.7-million contract to develop an open learning system and other projects for Universitas Terbuka and another $19.3 million for human resource development on the country's Eastern Islands.

Consultant services offered to foreign governments and corporations through the British Columbia public post-secondary system range from the establishment of high-technology computer training to instruction and instructor training in manufacturing and agriculture. Services can be as small as a $6,000 student

forestry training project in Burma or larger, such as the $2.5-million "Management Education, Economics, and Law" linkage between British Columbia and universities in China.

Public post-secondary education in the province of British Columbia ranks with the best in the world.

ABOVE: Photo courtesy, Lorraine Marigold
LEFT: Photo coutesy, Anne Wheeler

The province welcomes international students to enroll in university, college, and institute courses in the arts, sciences, and applied technologies in program areas where there is available capacity. To assist international students settle into their new surroundings, orientation is provided to such things as local transportation, establishing bank accounts, the postal system, telephone services, local shopping areas, and religious services available in the community.

Many overseas corporations have found it advantageous to send employees here for training in British Columbia technologies or to

Photos courtesy, Lorraine Marigold

invite British Columbian experts to their country to train employees and trainers. For instance, a huge construction conglomerate in Japan, an entrepreneurial trendsetter, is sending carpenters to British Columbia to learn the techniques of 2 by 4 frame construction, a fast-growing sector of Japan's home building market. To supplement their professional development campaign, this corporation has also inquired about hiring British Columbia instructors to teach on company premises in Japan.

In 1989 an ongoing program for management training was established under the auspices of the Canadian International Development Agency (CIDA) to provide training for the Institute for Development of Educational Administrators (IDEA), a residential institute in Thailand. Under this program, Thai administrators come to British Columbia to study, and experts from British Columbia colleges travel to Thailand to present seminars and workshops on educational administration.

In Indonesia, British Columbia consultants are assisting with Central Forestry Education and Training; in Singapore, programs are being co-operatively developed in CAD/CAM, Biomedical Electronics, Accounting, Financial Management, and English Language training.

British Columbia has a strong background in development of natural resources, and extensive training programs are available in modern resource management technologies. Resource development programs are continually being customized to meet the requirements of various international clients.

Business management training programs are also available, both at undergraduate and graduate levels. Services in this field can include initial needs assessments; research, design, and development of equipment and software; curriculum development; and ongoing project evaluation. There are joint research projects and a variety of training programs to meet the specific needs of international clients, all of which can be provided either in the province or in any country around the world.

Students come to British Columbia from all parts of the world to take advantage of these varied learning experiences. They can attend a post-secondary institution near a well-populated, cosmopolitan urban centre or in a more remote community surrounded by spectacular Canadian scenery. They can choose

to live in student quarters on campus or immerse themselves in Canadian customs by living with a local family. Recreation opportunities range from outdoor activities such as skiing, sailing, horseback riding, golf, and camping to sophisticated theatre, dining, and entertainment.

The universities provide opportunities for post-graduate studies in a wide range of fields. Colleges and institutes offer business, vocational, and technology-related career training and provide opportunities to complete university degrees. The colleges also offer a smaller, more personalized environment where students can study a chosen field while concurrently improving their English skills.

Multiculturalism in British Columbia has benefited the development of a large body of teachers, program planners, and curriculum developers who are highly skilled in providing English language training. All three universities have developed international reputations in applied linguistics, and most of the province's other public post-secondary institutions offer excellent English language programs.

Public post-secondary institutions in British Columbia are well aware that a cosmopolitan student body en-

Convinced of the value of international education, British Columbia's public post-secondary institutions are working hard to expand their programs of international study and research in Canada, to form joint ventures with educational institutions, business, and government in other

countries, and to locate opportunities for faculty and students to expand their education opportunities abroad.

As a way of achieving these goals, representatives of British Columbia institutions make personal visits to target countries and attend education conventions and trade shows to market the variety of programs offered by British Columbia's public post-secondary education system, and to deal with queries made directly to the institutions by international corporations.

Underlying the work of the province's public post-secondary institutions, the British Columbia

**ABOVE AND ABOVE RIGHT: Photos courtesy, Lorraine Marigold**
**RIGHT: Photo courtesy, Anne Wheeler**

riches the educational environment for the entire community. Mutually beneficial connections and long-term career development opportunities are nurtured in such an environment. Thus, both international and local students have the opportunity to become better informed and more active global citizens. Similarly, opportunities for faculty exchanges attract first-class instructors and enhance both their academic standing and the institution's programs.

Ministry of Advanced Education Training and Technology has supported these marketing efforts for a number of years. This support culminated in 1990 with the establishment of the British Columbia Centre for International Education (BCCIE) in Vancouver, an organization designed to facilitate, foster, and co-ordinate activities between provincial education institutions and overseas governments and corporations.

BCCIE manager Valerie Cottingham is building "a network of sources of information, opportunities, and expertise pertaining to international education and all of the players involved." As she explains, "International education is a huge and diverse area of activity so that it is virtually impossible for an individual to become conversant, let alone an expert, in all areas. Facilitating access to up-to-date information will be an

important role for the centre."

One of the centre's first responsibilities has been administration of the new British Columbia Asia Pacific Awards program, recently announced by the ministry to encourage and assist students interested in studying overseas and scholars interested in working overseas. The centre will also act as a clearinghouse for information on international opportunities in education and training, and as a forum for discussion of standard, issues, and trends in international education.

The BCCIE will strive to heighten both internal and external awareness of British Columbia's international education activities and will let the

appropriate people and institutions know what overseas opportunities are available to them. It is also willing to facilitate joint-venture projects in education or research, and co-operative development of quality, competitive project proposals for submission to international funding agencies.

Situated as it is on the Pacific Rim, it is vital that British Columbia become a capable, sophisticated partner in the rapidly developing Asia Pacific community. Connections established through the education system are expected to grow into positive international relationships in other sectors of the British Columbia economy, enabling the province to forge links between companies, governments, and educational institutions in Europe, Southeast Asia, and the United States. British Columbia invites all its neighbours in the Pacific Rim to benefit from the many opportunites, educational and otherwise, which can be obtained through association with this fast-growing province.

**Photos courtesy, Lorraine Marigold**

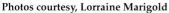

# Ministry of Development, Trade, and Tourism

The British Columbia Ministry of Development, Trade, and Tourism was established in response to the province's rapidly developing export economy and to investment interest from abroad.

Few places in the world offer the natural resources and strategic location available to investors in British Columbia, Canada's westernmost province. Poised on the Pacific Rim, with ready access across the American border, and strong cultural and ethnic ties both in Europe and in Asia, British Columbia provides an excellent gateway to global markets.

Investment opportunities in British Columbia are complemented by the province's moderate climate; stable government; large, skilled workforce; reliable energy sources; superior transportation and education systems; close free-trade ties with huge markets in the United States; and by the province's expanding economy.

Historically, British Columbia built its economic strength on a rich resource base—forestry, mining, fishing, water, energy, and land. As the province moves into the twenty-first century, a new, diversified economy is emerging, which includes rapidly growing aerospace and subsea technologies, an electronics industry, value-added forest products, fashion design, and the hospitality and tourism trades. In response to these excellent opportunities, queries have come in from investors around the world.

British Columbia recognizes that future growth and prosperity depend largely on attracting both capital and expertise on a global scale. At ministry offices in the World Trade Centre in Vancouver, market specialists for each geographic area of the globe serve as liaisons between foreign offices and British Columbia business people.

The ministry is also establishing a network of offices at key points. Currently, aside from their offices in Vancouver, Victoria, and Ottawa, Ontario, the province has international offices in Seattle, Los Angeles, London, Munich, Tokyo, Seoul, Hong Kong, and Singapore, a tourism office in San Francisco, and a British Columbia Trade Development Corporation sponsored office in Taiwan.

Perhaps one of the most important of the ministry initiatives is the for-

RIGHT: From British Columbia's large mining sector comes the raw materials for locally manufactured wire, cable, and machined metals.

BELOW: Beautiful Vancouver is nestled between the ocean and the mountains.

mation of the B.C. Trade Development Corporation (B.C. Trade) in 1989. B.C. Trade's mandate is to promote export, thus supplementing the initial work of the ministry. Corpo-

Abundant water resources fill the needs of agriculture, industry, and hydro-electric generation.

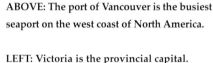

ABOVE: The port of Vancouver is the busiest seaport on the west coast of North America.

LEFT: Victoria is the provincial capital.

ration activities include sector-specific marketing, export counselling and training, and resource and information systems development. In its first 10 months of operation, B.C. Trade promoted an estimated $50-million worth of export sales, organized or participated in approximately 160 events, counselled more than 600 companies, provided financial sup-

port or loan guarantees for some 150 companies, received 100,000 inquiries or visits at its Business Information Centre, and expanded B.C. Business Network's on-line electronic database to include more than 900 companies and nearly 100 organizations.

Because of extensive knowledge gained from worldwide contacts, the ministry has been able to foster several other important initiatives. The B.C. International Commercial Arbitration Centre provides expertise in all areas of commerce, and the Europe 1992 Advisory Committee announced in February 1990 that it is providing two-way communication between government and industry in developing a viable European market.

The International Financial Centre, Vancouver, was a result of joint federal and provincial tax revisions that encourage completion in

Vancouver of international transactions. By August 1990 47 financial institutions had signed up and more agreements were in progress.

The joint federal-provincial Asia Pacific Initiative (API), established in 1987, completed its three-year mandate in March 1990. Before it was concluded, API had made recommendations in aerospace, tourism, hotel and culinary trades job training; studied the potential impact of expanding the Vancouver International Airport; and established a wide variety of multiculturalism projects.

If the British Columbia economy is any indication, the ministry's programs have been successful. The business immigration program, for instance, is designed to assist business immigrants who will contribute to the growth of the provincial economy and create jobs. In 1989, for example, unemployment actually dropped in British Columbia because 77,000 new jobs were created, the best job-creation performance of any province in Canada, and the best for British Columbia since 1981.

# The Roy Lisogar Story

From a White Spot carhop to a multi-million-dollar real estate developer, Roy Lisogar, son of an Alberta postmaster, has enjoyed an exciting and productive life.

While a student at King Edward High School in Vancouver, young Lisogar dreamed of one day owning a restaurant like his boss, Nat Bailey. Now he owns two hotels with Roy's Steak & Seafood House in the Century Plaza Hotel, Vancouver, and the Riverboat Restaurant in the Royal Towers Hotel, in New Westminster. However, to achieve this success he took a circuitous route.

**Century Plaza Hotel, the tallest building in Vancouver at the time of its construction, is the company flagship.**

Lisogar's first entrepreneurial venture resulted when by chance he met with Harry Thomas, a full-blooded Indian from Kamloops. A horse breaker, Thomas provided wild horses, and Lisogar produced Vancouver's first rodeo, held at Callister Park in 1943. The venture brought in $6,000.

Lisogar optimistically invested his money in the Windsor Hotel in Camrose, Alberta. Revenues did not cover expenses and within a year the mortgage company foreclosed. Roy Lisogar returned to Vancouver to work and to study at the University of British Columbia.

Instead in the ensuing years he worked for Boeing Aircraft as an illustrator, went to Hollywood where he performed as a stuntman, and organized the Canadian Ice Fantasy, an ice show that toured the continent for three years. At that time television was invented. Its popularity closed theatres, outdoor shows, and Lisogar's ice show. Lisogar married Lorrie Perkins, the star of his show and turned to other work.

During the early 1950s, he designed and renovated offices, restaurants, and hotels. While politicians and planners talked about doing it, Lisogar built Vancouver's first low-rent, family apartment, the Fraser Villa, designed by architect Gerald Hamilton. The modern 82-suite complex included stores, a swimming pool, and a good mix for family living. It was an instant success.

Lisogar's Construction Company went on to change the Vancouver sky-

**Roy Lisogar, owner of Lisogar Construction Company.**

line, building over $100 million worth of buildings, including more than 36 major developments in the Vancouver area. Examples include Hycroft Mews, the most deluxe condominium in British Columbia; Century Plaza Hotel, which was the tallest building in Vancouver at the time of its construction; and the Burrard Health Centre, one of the city's finest medical facilities.

Lisogar can even be proud of his least profitable project. In the mid-1960s he built a 30-suite senior citizens home and sold it to his favorite non-profit organization, the Ukranian Professional Businessman's Club, for one dollar. By 1988 Lisogar, 68 years old and in excellent health, had more than 400 employees. Then, at the high point of his career, tragedy struck. Lisogar had a major stroke and was forced to close his construction company.

Today Lisogar's two daughters with their husbands manage the hotels. Roy Lisogar and his wife have retired to their waterfront home in West Vancouver. For a hobby Lisogar is painting, a talent he excelled in during his early years.

# Coast Hotels

Established less than 20 years ago, Coast Hotels is already aspiring to become the only national chain with its roots in British Columbia. Coast has a network of 21 hotels across Canada through a variety of management and reservations agreements. Through affiliation with West Coast Hotels of Seattle, it also has connections on the American Pacific Coast and in Europe.

With a strong, international senior management team and major financial backing, this relatively young chain is now investigating expansion in the Prairie Provinces, Ontario, and Atlantic Canada.

Coast Hotels was started by the O'Neill family in 1972. The family had been known in the hospitality industry since 1959, when J.J. O'Neill established National Caterers. In 1972 O'Neill purchased the 50-room Gold River Chalet on Vancouver Island. O'Neill's oldest son, Robert, graduate of the food and hotel management program at the B.C. Institute of Technology, succeeded him as general manager.

Just before the recession in the early 1980s, Coast underwent major expansion, through purchase from the Delta chain of hotels in Campbell River, Prince George, and Kamloops.

Similar to most B.C. businesses, Coast found it hard to stay afloat during the early 1980s. National Caterers provided stability for the struggling company. Management continued to expand through managing properties owned by other investors. The firm took the lead as Canada's fastest-growing hotel chain during that time.

By 1987 Coast owned five proper-

*The Coast Victoria Harbourside Hotel offers 132 luxurious rooms and suites, each with a private balcony which offers a captivating view of Victoria's Inner Harbour.*

*The 267-room Coast Plaza at Stanley Park features 11 meeting rooms to suit groups of 10 to 450 as well as a picturesque garden terrace perfect for receptions.*

ties and managed eight. It had annual sales of $75 million and assets worth more than $25 million. In 1988 the Tokyo-based multinational Okabe Group purchased Coast Hotels, making a major investment which has enabled Coast to implement an ambitious expansion and diversification program for the future. It also purchased the Coast Plaza at Stanley Park, the former Ramada Renaissance and the Denman Place Mall for $45 million and began looking for more acquisitions.

Today Coast provides a network of first-class facilities located across Canada. Although its main client is the travelling businessperson, Coast also caters to leisure travellers and other market segments.

Opening in June 1991, the development of the 132-room hotel and 52-slip marina on the harbour in Victoria will be a key link in Coast Hotels western network.

Highlighting the company's move into Eastern Canada is the Hotels La Citadelle which will be the flagship of the eastern operation. This fine European-style hotel offers 180 deluxe rooms and suites at the centre of Montreal's business and cultural life.

In each region of the province, travellers will find a specialized Coast Hotel. A national network, convenient toll-free telephone reservation service, and good value for the money has made Coast one of B.C.'s most popular hotel chains. Coast is able to deliver a consistently high standard of service and hospitality throughout all Coast proper-

ties, retaining and building on the loyalty of guests.

In addition, much of its success is due to the chain's aggressive marketing program. Coast regularly conducts market research and engages in extensive marketing activities, such as national and regional advertising and sales promotions. A toll-free central reservations system doubled its sales between 1987 and 1990. Coast also services travel professionals throughout Canada and the United States with direct mail and trade show representation. With these techniques, Coast is working to increase occupancy and client loyalty for each property and the entire chain.

Although he has retired from the hotel chain, J.J. O'Neill is still involved in National Caterers. Rob O'Neill took over as president in 1988. Rob is a member of the Young President's Association.

The younger son, John, vice president of marketing, sales and development, is a commerce graduate of the University of British Columbia. He was named Hotelier of the Year by the Canadian Travel and Tourism Industry in 1989.

The chain has also participated in major community events. Coast Hotels provided accommodation for 1,000 broadcasters at the 1988 Winter Olympic Games in Calgary. The chain is also official hotel sponsor for Tourism B.C.'s Music '91 initiative, a promotion of the arts in small communities throughout the province.

# Pacific Press Limited

A new, state-of-the-art printing system has put Pacific Press Limited in Vancouver at the leading edge of publication technology. The cost-efficient, environmentally friendly plant was opened in Surrey in the spring of 1990. The Surrey site is ideal, providing a rapidly expanding population base, a central location, relatively inexpensive land, and room for future expansion.

Pacific Press, a member of the Southam Newspaper Group, publishes two Vancouver dailies. *The Province*, a morning tabloid, targets the readership of young professionals. *The Vancouver Sun,* an afternoon broadsheet paper, is aimed at families. Combined circulation of 440,000 makes Pacific Press the 14th-largest publisher in North America and the largest in British Columbia.

The Surrey facility, south of the Fraser River, enables the firm to distribute its papers more efficiently throughout the Fraser Valley, while the Vancouver plant continues to serve the areas north of the Fraser. The new plant, with its $13-million Flexoman system, will print 30,000 to 35,000 papers per hour when it reaches full capacity.

The municipality of Surrey was glad to welcome this modern plant. It enhances the tax base with minimal effect on its surroundings. The plant uses an environmentally friendly water-based ink that gives sharper reproduction—both in black and white and in color—and it does not rub off easily. Surplus ink is recycled. After the system is washed, the water is reused to dilute the black ink, and excess water is filtered before disposal to remove the last of the contaminants.

Even the air inside the plant is pure. Water-based ink does not mist like the oil-based inks, providing economy as well as maintaining air

quality. Filters on the presses collect all of the newsprint dust.

The Flexo system also uses less energy and less paper. A slightly smaller page—4 percent shrinkage each way—results in 7 percent less paper used and saves the company $1.5 million a year. In addition, Flexo printing wastes far less paper—both during start up and during the printing process.

The Surrey plant is primarily a production facility. Negatives of complete page layouts are sent by laser facsimile over 2.5 kilometres of dedicated phone lines from Vancouver. Two reader-writer fax sets transmit the page negatives at a res-

ABOVE CENTER: From the reporter on the beat to the doorstep of British Columbians. Photo by Ian Smith, *The Vancouver Sun*

ABOVE: Stu Noble (left), president of Pacific Press Limited, and Jerry Marr, director of planning and development, astride the last beam added to the new Surrey plant. Photo by Peter Hulbert, *The Province*

LEFT: Pacific Press' modern plant in Surrey, British Columbia, was officially opened in September 1990. Photo by Greg Osadchuk, *The Province*

olution of 1,000 lines per inch. It takes an average of four minutes to transmit the image and another four minutes to make the thin, plastic plates used for printing. These new plates are safer, easier to work with and less expensive than the old steel-backed plates.

Now a member of the Southam Newspaper Group, *The Vancouver Sun* and *The Province* have roots firmly set in British Columbia history and have grown along with this province. HeWitt Bostock established a paper called *The Weekly Province* in 1894 in Victoria. In 1898 the Klondike gold rush hit Vancouver and HeWitt moved his paper to the booming city. Because it was more readable, carried more current news, and directed its advertising at the Klondikers coming through town, *The Province* soon outstripped the other two Vancouver papers.

Walter Nichol bought *The Vancouver Daily Province* in 1904. In 1907 the paper experienced a business depression. At that time Nichol established a policy, still in effect today, of maintaining quality news, even at cost to other departments of the paper.

*The Province*'s competitors joined forces in 1912 to publish a morning paper called *The Sun*. Its history can be traced back to two papers, *The*

*Advertiser* and the *Daily News* which first published in 1886.

By 1917 *The Sun* was in financial difficulty. James Cromie purchased it in August 1917, and the Cromie family ran the paper for the next 40 years. Southam had purchased *The Province* in 1923, moved it into new premises at Hastings and Cambie in 1925, and still retains ownership. *The Sun* has been an evening paper since 1926. *The Province* switched to the morning field in 1957. *The Sun* published morning and evening editions off and on until 1946.

In 1963 FP Publications bought the Sun Publishing Company. In January 1980 Thompson Newspapers Limited bought *The Vancouver Sun*, and in August of the same year sold it and its shares in Pacific Press Ltd. to Southam Inc.

When Southam purchased *The Sun* from Thompson Newspapers in 1980, the Kent Commission was appointed to investigate the implications of a single corporation owning both of the city's major papers. The commission ruled that each paper must maintain independent news and editorial departments.

Pacific Press Ltd. was formed in May 1957, owned jointly by Southam Inc., and Sun Publishing Co. Each continued to appoint its own publisher, but the physical assets of the papers were taken over by Pacific Press Ltd. New premises at 2250 Granville were occupied in December 1965.

Each jealously guarded its own territory. Stuart Noble, chief executive officer for the group, has worked on breaking down some of these walls. Each paper has its own editor-in-chief, and the news and editorial de-

partments remain separate. However, cost efficiency and improved customer service have been achieved by combining the advertising departments. A joint public relations department has also been a good move. Although both papers had their ups and downs, they have become the province's main providers of news, opinion, advertising, and information.

Noble emphasizes that the employees are the key to business success. Although both papers have had a history of labor strife, there are also a lot of long-term employees with the companies. A new policy and procedures manual emphasizes the commitment to development of a spirit of co-operation and teamwork.

The Industrial Relations Management Association presented Noble with an Award of Merit for significant achievement in Human Relations Management in B.C. in 1987-1988. But he thinks there is still a lot of work to be done.

Since its formation in 1957, Pacific Press Limited has grown with the booming B.C. population. The Surrey presence positions them well for maintaining customer service as B.C.'s expanding population moves across the Fraser River and into the valley.

Despite a slowing of the B.C. economy, particularly some bad signs from the forestry industry, Noble remains optimistic. Vancouver has a key location near expanding Pacific Rim markets. The B.C. population continues to grow, and as land in the city core fills and becomes more expensive, people are moving to the Fraser Valley.

"Pacific Press will try to keep up with the population," says Noble. "The Surrey location, central to B.C.'s Lower Mainland, positions the company well for efficient customer service and future growth."

# Northwest Sports Enterprises Ltd.

A strong hockey team, similar to any other business, depends on a strong economy for profitability and growth. British Columbia's economy has grown rapidly in recent years, and Arthur Griffiths, president of Northwest Sports Enterprises Ltd., declares that it is time for the Vancouver Canucks hockey team to catch up.

Northwest Sports Enterprises, owner of the Canucks, declared revenue of more than $23 million in 1989, and the team brought an estimated $50-million worth of business into the local economy from fans and visiting teams. The National Hockey League draft was held in Vancouver for the first time in the spring of 1990.

British Columbia first became involved with national hockey in 1915, when the Vancouver Millionaires challenged the Ottawa Senators for possession of its recently won Stanley Cup. The Senators promptly boarded a train to meet this challenge from an unknown team. In the first Stanley Cup playoffs west of Winnipeg, the upstart Vancouver team trounced the Senators 6-2, 8-3, and 12-3. Vancouver then proved its mettle by qualifying for the Stanley Cup finals five times in the ensuing nine years.

Seven thousand wildly cheering fans, nearly 7 percent of the population, attended the 1915 game, and each of the winning players took home a whopping $300. Today the Vancouver Canucks play in an arena with twice that much seating serving nearly 14 times the 1915 population, and 15 NHL players earn more than one million dollars a year.

As part of the Western Hockey League, the team won the Patterson cup four times. Then the NHL decided to double in size in 1966. Vancouver residents confidently felt

ABOVE: A pair of 19s in action as Petr Nedved of the Canucks tries to elude Rod Brind'Amour of St. Louis.

ABOVE RIGHT: Vancouver's goaltending sensation Troy Gamble deals with Edmonton's Craig Simpson.

RIGHT: Canuck forward Greg Adams, who led his club with 30 goals last season, manoeuvres around Chicago defenceman.

they qualified for a franchise, and when this Canadian city was passed over in favor of six teams from the United States, outraged Canadian fans forced the league to reconsider, and Vancouver was granted NHL standing on May 22, 1970. At that time the Pacific Coliseum was just two years old, and adequate to serve Vancouver's population of 430,000.

After formal organization of national hockey, Vancouver played in the Western League until 1970, when the team's bid for a $6-million NHL franchise was finally accepted. The Griffith family was given the opportunity to purchase the team in 1974 when the Medacor, one of the major investors in the franchise, experienced financial difficulties. Thus the Canucks became a subsidiary of Western Broadcasting. As the two companies grew, diverse administra-

tive requirements made it necessary to develop Northwest Sports Enterprises Ltd. as a separate entity.

For the Canucks to remain competitive, they need strong community support—but this is hard to achieve with an arena that is the third smallest in the National Hockey League, serving a population exceeding 1.34 million. It is impossible to accommodate the full spectrum of fans with the 15,700 seats available. Northwest Sports Enterprises Ltd. is working on a three-step solution, the essential first step being a new, larger arena with facilities for all levels of clients. Such a facility is near at hand. Once adequate facilities are available, Arthur Griffiths plans to implement aggressive marketing to renew community support and bring in the cash necessary to build a stronger, more consistent league-leading team.

# Patrons

The following individuals, companies, and organizations have made a valuable commitment to the quality of this publication. Windsor Publications and The British Columbia Chamber of Commerce greatfully acknowledge their participation in *British Columbia: Land of Rich Diversity.*

Andersen Consulting
B.C. Ministry of Environment
B.C. Pavilion Corporation
B.C. Round Table on Environment
    and Economy
British Columbia Telephone
    Company (B.C. Tel)
Coast Hotels
Dairyland Foods
Ebco Industries Ltd.
The Roy Lisogar Story
Ministry of Advanced Education,
    Training, and Technology-
    International Education
Ministry of Development, Trade, and
    Tourism
Northwest Sports Enterprises Ltd.
Pacific Press Limited
Seaboard Life Insurance Company
Wedgewood
Williams Moving & Storage
Women's Programs

# Bibliography

B.C. Central Credit Union, Economics Department. "Economic Analysis of British Columbia." Vol. 10, No. 1, February 1990.

B.C. Film Commission. "On Location in Your Neighborhood."

B.C. Ministry of Tourism and Provincial Secretary, Research Services Branch. "Report: 1988 Highlights."

B.C. Transit. *Transitions: One Hundred Years of Transit in British Columbia, 1890-1990*. n.d.: n.p.

*BC Discovery*. "Discussions with Dr. Denis Connor." May/June 1990.

British Columbia Ferry Corporation. "Annual Report 1989-1990."

British Columbia Forest Service. "All Things Considered—Forest Management in British Columbia."

Council of Forest Industries of British Columbia. "British Columbia Forest Industry Fact Book—1989."

Fisheries Council of British Columbia/Price Waterhouse. "The Economic Impacts of Fishing in British Columbia—1988 and 1989."

Fisheries Council of British Columbia. "Trends in the Commercial Fishing Industry of British Columbia—1983-1987."

Greater Vancouver Regional District. "Creating Our Future." July 1990.

Hudson, D.J. "Speech to the Prospectors and Developers Association of Canada, March 14, 1990."

Mining Association of British Columbia/Price Waterhouse. "Mining in British Columbia—1988."

Schreiner, John. "The Port of Vancouver." *Canadian Geographic*. August/September 1987.

Science Council of British Columbia. "SPARK Report: Forestry Research and Development in British Columbia—A Vision for the Future."

Science Council of British Columbia. "SPARK Report: Science and Technology: Its Impact on the B.C. Economy—a Twelve Year Plan."

Transport Canada. "Vancouver International Airport, Annual Review, Year Ended March 31, 1990."

Transport Canada. "Vancouver International Airport, Parallel Runway Project—Environmental Impact Statement." August 1990.

Vancouver Port Corporation. "Port of Prince Rupert—1989 Statistical Synopsis; Port of Vancouver: Canada's Front Door on the Pacific."

Vancouver Stock Exchange. "Annual Report, 1989/90." *Vancouver Sun*. "Future Growth: Future Shock." (seven-part series). November 1990.

# Index